REAL-LIFE
RESUMÉS
THAT WORK!

REAL-LIFE RESUMÉS THAT WORK!

ON-LINE RESOURCES & JOB-WINNING RESUMÉS

From the World's Leading Career Consulting Firm

DRAKE BEAM MORIN

EDITED BY BOB STIRLING AND PAT MORTON

DBM
PUBLISHING

A DIVISION OF DRAKE BEAM MORIN, INC.

NEW YORK

ACKNOWLEDGMENTS

A number of individuals were quite generous with their insights, comments, and other assistance throughout this project. Among those most helpful were Cy Callahan, Carol DuBose, Judy Estrin, George Enoch, Jim McGovern, Ginny Rehberg, and Alice Snell.

CONTENTS

INTRODUCTION

Finding a position in today's economic climate has become a skill that no one can afford to be without. Today's rules are dramatically different from just a few years ago. Job security is a thing of the past. Skills, accomplishments, and flexibility count more than ever. Companies once thought of as invincible have become the new casualties of global competition.

The result is that the restructuring of business and the continued downsizing within many of the nation's top companies have thrust workers of all ages, occupations, and income levels into a highly competitive job market. And people who once thought they'd never have to look for another position are, in fact, in the job market.

Those employers who are hiring are looking for marketing materials—resumés and cover letters—that show high levels of achievement, cost-consciousness, and innovative ideas. They're looking for professionals with a wide range of skills in many areas, and accomplishments are increasingly taking precedence over experience in today's fast-paced world.

Because succeeding in today's job market requires more sophistication and know-how than in the past, effective marketing materials are vitally important to the search process. These materials form your image. You need to think of yourself as the product—a product with much to offer. Your job is to develop a targeted campaign that promotes your talents and effectively markets your skills to potential employers.

This book is designed to give you the edge you need to succeed in your search. It will help you develop the tools essential for marketing yourself more effectively. It will help you tailor your materials to your audience by providing you with samples of resumés specific to hot industries. And it will open new markets to you by giving you up-to-date lists of on-line job resources—with the additional information you need to use this technology most efficiently.

You can have confidence in the guidance and information provided here, because this book draws on Drake Beam Morin's vast experience in career and human resources management consulting. Over the past 30 years, DBM has helped over a million people develop successful job search campaigns.

Many of DBM's experts have shared their expertise and insights in an effort to provide a realistic and up-to-date assessment of what employers expect. The sample marketing materials contained in this book are modeled after real-life examples that have been used by DBM candidates to find new work in all kinds of employment situations.

We hope that this book provides a new focus for your marketing campaign. And most of all, we hope that it helps you succeed.

1
THE RESUMÉ

THE PURPOSE OF A RESUMÉ

A good resumé acts like a good advertisement, enticing the reader to learn more about you through personal contact. It should include only the facts and features—the selling points—that are relevant to the reader's interests and needs.

The primary purpose of a resumé is to stimulate prospective employers' interest in meeting you, and in arranging a personal interview. Notice that "stimulating interest" is not the same as "telling everything" about yourself. In fact, the more detail you put into your resumé, the more likely it is that a busy screener of candidates will notice an item that could exclude you from the hiring process.

Think of your resumé package as a sales document that illustrates your skills and experience. It should be written clearly and concisely, outlining the pertinent information that illustrates your qualifications for the position.

A good resumé should:

1. Act as a "door opener" that makes companies want to investigate your qualifications further.
2. Inform your network contacts about your career background so that they can assist in your search.
3. Serve as a leave-behind at the end of an informational interview.
4. Provide a framework for discussion during a face-to-face interview.
5. Satisfy the requirements of search firms and advertisers.

1

Remember, there are many ways to stimulate people's interest in you besides distributing resumés, such as marketing letters and personal contacts. The resumé is not the leading edge of your job search; it is more often a follow-up device. Certainly, it is no substitute for personal contact.

Your resumé is part of your image; it needs to be interesting, concise, and visually attractive. But to prepare the most effective resumé, you first need to know your audience.

RESUMÉ READERS

There are several types of resumé readers: those who screen resumés as part of their professional duties, executives who screen resumés as part of the hiring process, and other friends and contacts who see your materials during the course of your job search.

The first category includes search consultants and their staffs at executive search firms, employment agencies and their staffs, as well as internal employment managers and recruiters who work directly for hiring companies.

These professionals agree on a few basic principles about resumés:

- Resumés should be clear, succinct, direct, and presented in an attractive, easy-to-read format.
- Resumés should include a summary, so that screeners can quickly match the applicant with their needs.
- Resumés should provide complete employment histories without unexplained gaps.
- Resumés should be polished and interesting.

People who handle many resumés are looking for clarity, brevity, and directness. They want to know right away the type of work you seek, then they scan for a quick impression of your qualifications. In this way, they can quickly match you with their search assignments or openings. Typically, they will take only a few seconds to decide whether to read the whole resumé. Even then they may take only a minute or two to read it through.

They will be attracted to a polished resumé that presents the information in an interesting way. But they will be put off by a resumé that appears unconventional or designed to conceal facts, as well as irritated by a resumé that is difficult to read.

Bear in mind that the objective of resumé screeners is to eliminate candidates. They're looking for an excuse to toss your resumé. They will discard sloppy or dull resumés as well as those containing anything that appears negative or that diverges from what they are seeking. Conversely, they will tend to home in on experience that seems congruent with their current job placement needs.

Another potential audience is the actual executive or decision maker who might be interested in you or who might interview you. Some decision makers like to glance through resumés themselves, if only to keep up with the current job seekers. These non-professional readers tend to be very susceptible to immediate first impressions. Your success with them may depend on whether they see some experience or personal trait that fits with their personal vision of the "ideal" employee.

They may struggle with the decision of whether to call you on the phone, have someone down the line check you out, or write to you for further information. Most of them have never been trained to conduct interviews. They may not be skilled in questioning techniques, and they may need the resumé in their hands to know what to discuss during the interview.

Another category of readers includes the friends and personal contacts you are enlisting as your helpers and personal consultants in your job campaign. Even though these people know you personally, they probably don't remember your complete history, much less your job-related strengths and accomplishments. Therefore, your resume will help them to to become familiar with your skills and to suggest other contacts that might be helpful in your search.

Discourage your friends and contacts from handing out your resumé too freely. You may lose control of who is getting them, as well as lose the chance to follow up with a phone call or interview in a timely manner.

You may be sure that your resume will not please everyone. Nonetheless, it's worthwhile to solicit comments or feedback from various readers before finalizing your resumé.

RESUMÉ FORMATS

The two most common types of resumé formats are chronological and functional. The chronological resumé emphasizes your employment record—where you worked and for how long, your job titles, your responsibilities, and your accomplishments. Your jobs are listed in reverse order, the most recent coming first.

The functional resumé emphasizes the kinds of work you've done, the skills you have, and your accomplishments in various aspects of business. It organizes work experience by business functions, such as general marketing, management, production, finance, or any of their subfunctions—or by skills. It usually incorporates a range of accomplishments to illustrate expertise in a particular skill area or field of business.

The chronological resumé is by far the most commonly used. Therefore, it is what most recruiting people and seasoned interviewers expect to see. The functional resumé is more adaptable to special problems in the job search. For example, if your employment history has been erratic or suggests "job-hopping," you may want to de-emphasize this by talking first about your functional skills and accomplishments. If you are planning to make a radical career change, you will need to de-emphasize aspects of your experience and try to highlight your more relevant skills and knowledge. And, if you are re-entering the job market after a long absence, you will want to emphasize your skills and knowledge.

However, the functional resumé may irritate resumé screeners because it appears to conceal what they are accustomed to looking for. But if you are one of those special cases who needs a functional resumé, you'll probably be aiming at a different target anyway—the decision maker.

Ideally, each type of resumé incorporates elements of the other. The chronological resumé becomes more meaningful when you list specific accomplishments under each job. A functional resumé should usually include a condensed employment history (company, date, and job title). Worksheets for both formats, as well as a combination format, which features an abbreviated job history and a separate list of functional accomplishments, appear on the following pages.

In addition to these two formats, there are others that fit special situations. In the academic world, the emphasis may be on educational background and published papers. In fields such as publishing or public relations, a resumé might have a narrative style or show a creative flair. A law firm will require a very specialized format, and a public accounting firm might expect a very formal, conservative type of resumé.

Your resumé should show your versatility. Resumés that stress only one skill can often pigeon-hole a job candidate. If you're coming from a big corporate environment and were exposed to a wide range of experience, you may even wish to consider multiple resumés to better target your skills in specific areas.

The key is to tailor your resumé and other marketing materials to the requirements of your career objective. You may want to use a combination of formats that can serve to better reflect your individual skills and accomplishments. You may also want to highlight your skills by using a "key word" format in which you present pertinent skills set off in columns or in a summary. Your keyword profile can include a listing of functions and tasks in which you are skilled, or highlight management and people skills.

FUNCTION/SKILL KEYWORDS	MANAGEMENT/PEOPLE SKILL KEYWORDS
Budgeting	Culture Change
Cost Control	Change Management
Energy Management	Organizational Alignment
Facilities Management	Process Reengineering
Fire/Safety Systems	Turnaround Operations
Housekeeping	Performance Management
Office Services	Downsizing
Operations	Personal Coaching
Preventative Maintenance	Facilitation
Project Management	Team Building
Property Lease Management	Leadership
Purchasing	TQM
Security	360 Degree Feedback
Staff Supervision	Succession Planning
Team Player/Builder	Upward Appraisal
Vendor/Contractor Management	

Review the samples provided in chapter 4 for ideas. Just remember that the best resumés blend accomplishments with experience in a quick, easy-to-read format.

Keeping these guidelines in mind, you can use the worksheets on the following pages to develop your own chronological and functional resumés.

Resumé Components

THE SUMMARY

The summary explains in a few lines who you are and summarizes your credentials, skills, and qualifications for particular positions or functions. The summary should be 3 to 6 lines long, highlighting your career to date. Begin with your generic title, years of experience, and industry. Then outline your strengths and skills. If your list of skills is longer than one paragraph, you may want to use a bulleted "key word" format. You may also wish to include any positive personal traits that reflect on your ability to get the job done as well as any pertinent achievements and awards. However, these last two items are optional.

Word your summary to convey both your objectives and your major skills and qualifications. Another way of broadly identifying where you could fit in to the

Name
Address
City, State, Zip
Telephone Number

SUMMARY

_____

_____

WORK EXPERIENCE

Company _____ City/State _____ Dates Employed _____

Brief description of company (*optional*) _____

Job Title _____ Dates _____

Scope of responsibilities _____

Accomplishments _____

_____

Company _____ City/State _____ Dates Employed _____

Brief description of company (*optional*) _____

Job Title _____ Dates _____

Scope of responsibilities _____

Accomplishments _____

_____

EDUCATION AND TRAINING

Degree/Major _____

School (City, State) _____

OTHER (*optional*)

Publications _____

Professional memberships _____

Community involvement _____

Name
Address
City, State, Zip
Telephone Number

SUMMARY

_____

_____

MAJOR ACCOMPLISHMENTS

(Function 1)

_____

_____

(Function 2)

_____

_____

(Function 3)

_____

_____

WORK EXPERIENCE

Company _____ City, State _____ Dates Employed _____

Brief description of company (*optional*) _____

Job Title _____ Dates _____

Job Title _____ Dates _____

Company _____ City, State _____ Dates Employed _____

Brief description of company (*optional*) _____

Job Title _____ Dates _____

Job Title _____ Dates _____

EDUCATION AND TRAINING

Degree/Major _____

School (City, State) _____

OTHER (*optional*)

Publications _____

Professional memberships _____

Community involvement _____

Name
Address
City, State, Zip
Telephone Number

KEYWORDS OR SUMMARY

_____

_____

PROFESSIONAL EXPERIENCE

_____ , _____   _____
(PRESENT/LAST COMPANY) City, State   (Overall dates employed)

_____   _____
(Job Title)   (Dates)

_____ , _____   _____
(PRESENT/LAST COMPANY) City, State   (Overall dates employed)

_____   _____
(Job Title)   (Dates)

MAJOR ACCOMPLISHMENTS

_____
(FUNCTION)

- _____
- _____
- _____

_____
(FUNCTION)

- _____
- _____
- _____

EDUCATION

_____
(Degree awarded and major field)

_____
(School, City, State)

PROFESSIONAL DEVELOPMENT
(Course title, Provider)

OTHER (optional)
_____
(Special Awards/Professional Memberships/Community Leadership)

_____

_____

PERSONAL (Optional, only if it adds value)

potential employer's company is to include key words in your summary to suggest the positions and/or functions in which you are interested.

If you are in mid-career or later, be wary of over-emphasizing experience (e.g., "over 29 years of experience in tax management"). You could potentially convey a negative "age" message—or that you have stayed in one place too long.

Example:

Proven engineering/maintenance manager with extensive experience in directing facilities planning, building, and expansion projects ranging in scope from $50,000 to $9 million. Achieved a reputation for aggressively completing projects on time and within budget. Implemented and later computerized maintenance and calibration of manufacturing and facilities equipment/structures with an annual budget of $2 million.

Example:

Administrative support professional with 10 years of multi-industry experience in Query Management Facilities (QMF/SQL) and Computerized Maintenance Management Systems (COMMS/CICS) supporting a sophisticated controlled/predictive maintenance work order system. Major strengths include organizing, planning, interpersonal skills, report writing, and training. Reputation as a team player and highly motivated self-starter.

Example:

Experienced project manager in the chemical industry, with achievements in design and manufacturing engineering. Background includes a Master's degree in Chemical Engineering from the University of Ottawa, as well as a 3-year assignment in corporate headquarters as a Staff Manufacturing Representative.

Since most resumé screeners decide in a matter of seconds whether they will read more than a few lines of a resumé, be sure that your summary matches the reader's needs and is interesting enough to warrant further review.

EMPLOYMENT HISTORY/WORK EXPERIENCE/CAREER BACKGROUND

For more recent jobs (those held within the past 10 years), it is reasonable to list each job assignment within each organization. Include dates of employment, followed by the company name and a one-sentence description of the scope of the company (e.g., annual sales, number of employees, principal products or services). Then, give your job title, followed by a sentence describing your responsibilities. If possible, include figures, such as annual sales, number of subordinates, or the size of the territory.

After each recent job, append some of your most impressive and applicable accomplishments, specifying the action you took and the result of that action quantified in percentages and dollars wherever possible. The amount of detail for each job should diminish as you reach further back. (Jobs of more than 10 to 15 years ago can be summarized in a single line.)

Example:

Professional Experience

Centennial Bank, N.A., Rochester, NY   1988–Present
Vice President and Manager, Check Processing

Directed staff of 175 and administered $8.75 million annual budget for premier check-clearing bank in a Federal Reserve District.

- Reduced expenses by 3.5 percent each year for three consecutive years while volume grew at 5 percent rate, resulting in net revenue improvement of $150,000 each month.

- Directed hardware and software conversion from Unisys to IBM with multiple software systems with minimum downtime or loss of productivity.

- Implemented work measurement throughout division to accurately reflect individual performance. Key indicator of success for this program was low 12 percent turnover rate.

Vice President and Manager, Data Processing Operations   1988–1993

Managed staff, equipment, and software to support data processing requirements in a dual mainframe, large IBM-system environment. Specific functions included:

Systems Programming	Computer Operations	Data Entry
Telecommunications	Systems Support	Data Base
Distributed Systems	Remote Operations	PCs

Reduced overall expenses by 10 percent and subsequently kept expenses flat.

EDUCATION/TRAINING

Unless you are looking for a position in academia, where your educational background will be of paramount interest, a summary of your education should be included on the last page of your resumé.

List your most current formal degree or diploma, then the next most current, down to the least current. Each notation should include the degree, the discipline or major, and the name and location of the institution. Note that the dates of education and degrees do not need to be included. They may provide a clue to age which could be used to discriminate.

This is also a good place to list supplementary training you have received, such as workshops, conferences, seminars, and special courses. In addition, list any licenses or certificates you've earned. You may also wish to highlight relevant academic credentials, honors, and any related academic extra-curricular activities.

Example:

Education

Master's of Business Administration—Health Care Management
City College, Portland, Oregon

Bachelor of Arts—Business Administration
City College, Portland, Oregon

MEMBERSHIPS/PUBLICATIONS

Information related to memberships in professional organizations and/or published materials related to your field is an added asset to any resumé. Guest speaking also adds to your credibility, especially lectures in your field of study or before organizations related to your area of expertise. However, avoid including details that are not relevant to your career objective.

Example (Health Care Industry):

Professional Affiliations

Licensed Nursing Home Administrator
American College of Health Care Administrators

Example (Academic Field):

Publications

How to Get the Most from VDTs, Aetna Life & Casualty, 1990 and annually thereafter.
"The Changing Role of the Systems Professional," DPMA Newsletter, Spring 1995.
"Color Use: A Rationale," with Richard J. Telesca, DPMA Newsletter, Fall 1994.
"Debunking Office Technology Myths," with Emmet J. McTeague, National Underwriter, Feb. 12, 1994.

PERSONAL DATA/COMMUNITY INVOLVEMENT

Personal data should only be included if it is either extraordinarily interesting—and will make the reader want to know more—or demonstrates a special skill. For example, you may have successfully coordinated a major fund-raising project in your community, demonstrating some marketing skills not shown in your work experience. Be sure that what you include here is relevant to the position you're seeking; otherwise, omit the section entirely.

MILITARY EXPERIENCE

If you've served in the military, set up a separate page as an addendum to your resumé with details covering your tour of duty and your accomplishments. Do you have any special skills because of your military experience? Perhaps you speak a foreign language fluently or have a particular affinity for working with computers. Detail any specific training received in that specialty. Then note the years of experience you've had working in that area and your level of expertise. Also list any accomplishments related to this skill.

REFERENCES

Do not include a line about references on your resumé, and don't offer them until they are asked for. You will know when the time is right, based on the seriousness of your negotiations, and you should be prepared to deliver your list at that time.

Depending on your length of service and the number of companies you have worked for in recent years, you may want to have three to six references available. Your most recent boss is an obvious choice, but don't hesitate to call on earlier bosses or someone at a higher level who may have a better impression of you. Some companies would like to have the names of one or two peers or associates who worked closely with you. Occasionally, they will ask for character references from non-work acquaintances or friends.

Ask the people you intend to list as references for permission to do so, and prepare them to be contacted by your prospective companies. Inform them of the nature of the job that is under consideration, as well as how you have positioned yourself to fit the job. This will give the reference some time to think about what to say in support of your marketing effort.

Many reference inquiries are now handled by telephone. Most companies are very guarded about what they will say in a letter; they usually confine their references to your dates of employment and the position held. In any event, try to get clarification on what the company's representatives will say in response to inquiries.

EXECUTIVE PROFILES

Many high-level professionals also develop an "Executive Profile" which includes such information as career highlights and a brief summary of professional affiliations. Also known as "bios," these are used most frequently at senior levels. They are designed to quickly summarize skills and accomplishments. They are more common in certain fields such as academia, publishing, government, and healthcare.

Most profiles read like the introduction of a guest speaker. The idea is to blend accomplishments and experience in a statement that reveals how the candidate is exceptional in his or her field. Most are written in a third-person narrative style.

When should you consider using an executive bio?

- When you are at a senior level in your field.
- If you are very accomplished in your field. For example, if you are a leading authority in your profession or if your work has been extensively published.
- When you wish to highlight significant achievements, such as the turnaround of a division, the introduction of several important products, or a breakthrough in science or medicine.

SPECIAL SITUATIONS

STARTING AT THE BOTTOM

Newcomers to any field must contend with the dilemma that bedevils all entry-level candidates—how do you get hired in a business world that wants experienced people? Many people find themselves in this position: recent high school and college graduates, foreign-born immigrants with no local experience, and those returning to the workforce after long sabbaticals.

There's no easy solution to this problem, but there are ways around it. How can you compete with other candidates who have more experience? Let your cover letter go to work for you. Talk about your education and training and how they have prepared you for your profession. Be specific about your intentions. Tell the employer exactly what you're looking for. Talk about what you bring to the party and how your skills will benefit the employer.

If you are a recent college graduate, most experts recommend listing your educational background first, followed by work experience, even if it's not directly related to your field. Screeners look at entry-level resumés to see what kinds of experiences you've had, levels of responsibility, and how much work you've juggled while going to school.

If you have professional experience in your particular field—as a summer intern, in a work-study program, or as a volunteer in your community—tell the screener what you've done. Give the dates, job titles, and responsibilities. Experience in the field can be your strongest asset.

Finally, computer skills are becoming increasingly important in today's highly literate work environment. If you are well-versed in software used in your profession, list it on your resumé.

Most entry-level jobs today are obtained through networking. Your best resources are your friends, family, and associates. Everybody has been through this before and knows what you're experiencing. The more people who know about your job search, the more likely your search will be a fruitful one.

TRANSFERRING YOUR SKILLS

Transferring your skills to another field or industry offers much of the same challenge as seeking an entry-level job, even if you already have significant professional experience in a certain field.

There could be a number of reasons for exploring a field where your credentials and experience may not immediately seem applicable. Certainly, if your recent work has been unsatisfying or if your industry is depressed, you have a special incentive to look into a new field. If you do, you need to balance your enthusiasm against the practicalities and the realities of the job market.

Look for industries or positions that are related to your skills and knowledge. For example, the field of banking has the following characteristics:

- It is a service industry, financial in nature.
- "Production" consists of processing great quantities of data and handling large volumes of paper.
- The personnel needs of banking consist of a great many entry-level workers, which present challenges in selection, training, retention, pay, etc.

Thus, your challenge is to find other industries that have similar circumstances and problems, where your bank-related skills could easily be transferred. Here are some possibilities—savings and loan, credit card operations, insurance, brokerage houses, and consumer credit.

If much of your experience has been in a certain function of business, like human resources, accounting, or sales, you may reason that you could fulfill your function in any industry. That may well be true, but sometimes individuals within the business world take a narrower vision; that is, a bank seeking a new Human Resources manager may tend to favor a candidate with considerable banking experience. This is an instance where you will need to emphasize skills more than experience in your marketing approach.

Some functions of business seem to be easier to sell across industry barriers—corporate attorney, patent department manager, deep water transportation expert, traffic manager, EDP operations manager, corporate aviation head. These are all somewhat specialized in their fields, no matter what the main business of their company may be. And remember, key management skills can be realigned into most functions and types of organizations.

If you are already in your mid- or late-career years, you may find some prejudice against a transfer of skills. However, strong skills can still be transferred into environments where experience and maturity are valued, although a bit more patience and very careful targeting may be required.

You can see that this sort of "creative targeting" requires visualizing where your skills could be transferred, in-depth knowledge of the business world, and development of new marketing strategies. Following are three examples of individuals who made successful transitions to entirely new careers by way of skill transfer.

Director, National Field Operations for the corporate headquarters of a major insurance company. He had spent 18 years with the company and had lived in six different cities as the company promoted him and moved him and his family. Based on his knowledge of operations and familiarity with relocation issues, he became Vice President, National Sales for a large well-known national *moving* company.

Facilities and Logistics Planning, manufacturing company. An avid fishing enthusiast, he originally wanted to open a fishing tackle store but abandoned that idea after working in one for a summer. Instead, he runs fishing expeditions out of a sports and outdoor retail store, using his skills in planning and logistics to set up and manage itineraries and movement of people on these trips.

Information Systems executive with an interest in cooking. He took his severance and savings and three months time to enroll in a culinary institute in France, then came back to the U.S. and apprenticed in a restaurant for six months. He has now opened his own Patisserie specializing in "distinctive cakes and pastries."

Remember that if you identify and talk about yourself in terms of past titles, functions, and experience, your range of possible future positions is likely to be limited to the same or similar industry/function. On the other hand, if you do a thorough job of identifying your managerial and technical skills, your traits, personality, and style, as well as give concrete examples in your marketing materials, you will widen the spectrum of your career choices and enhance your networking activities.

RESUMÉ DO'S AND DON'TS

Your resumé reflects your professionalism. Follow this list of do's and don'ts—based on the feedback of many resumé readers—to be sure that you make the best possible first impression:

DO

- Use parallel sentence structure.
- Punctuate your sentences correctly.
- Save capital letters for proper nouns.
- Spell out numbers where appropriate.
- Spell out abbreviations when they first appear.
- Check your spelling and grammar.
- Create visual interest by using short paragraphs, bullets, and white space.
- Use an 11 or 12 point font for text to ensure readability.
- Use a slightly larger font for headings so they stand out.
- Create a hierarchy of information.
- Use an attractive layout and high-quality paper.
- Present yourself accurately and positively.
- Include a summary statement.
- Include your most relevant accomplishments.
- Quantify your accomplishments.
- Use action-oriented words.
- Highlight responsibilities with bullets to emphasize your skills.
- Include your complete employment history—or at least the last 10 years.
- Have someone else proofread your resumé before it is printed.

DON'T

- Overuse highlighting techniques such as bold and italics.
- Give the same weight to both a heading and a company name.
- Be unnecessarily wordy.
- Use "I," "me," "my," and "we."
- Underline—it clutters the page.
- Smudge your resumé with fingerprints.
- Use long, complicated sentences, jargon, or "buzz words."
- Include your desired salary.

- Include references or even state that they are available on request.
- Bore your reader with too much information.
- Make your resumé more than two pages.

To get a clearer idea of the impression you'll make, ask yourself these questions when you're reviewing your resumé:

1. Is it interesting? Am I enjoying reading it?
2. Is it clear and direct?
3. Is it comprehensive of relevant information without being exhaustive?
4. Is it accurate and honest?
5. Does it "invite" the reader to find out more about me?
6. Do my accomplishments support my career objective?
7. Am I impressed?
8. Would I hire the person on that resumé?

2
USING ON-LINE RESOURCES

OVERVIEW

Dialing into on-line information services from your computer has become almost commonplace and demand for useful information on-line is way up and growing rapidly.

Among the most popular kinds of information appearing on-line are job and talent services—and not just for "techies." This chapter reveals concrete opportunities for anyone seeking to advance his or her career.

The on-line information boom is arriving in a variety of formats for matching task to talent, and talent to task. Resumé databases, on-line job postings, specialized bulletin-board services and electronic job-and-career research resources are powerful tools for the job-seeker, or those in the throes of a career transition.

Career planning has assumed a new importance in today's unstable job climate. No longer will most individuals pursue a linear career path. Instead they'll face plenty of choices and changes along the way. Ambitious—and prepared—individuals who can exploit all available resources will be more adaptable when change occurs (and it will).

Just as important, computer skills and knowledge of on-line sources developed while job-searching can be applied to other tasks, making you more valuable in the job market.

On-line employment-related services are covering more industries and functions at all levels. In addition to opportunity-hunting, computer-literate job-seekers can network with colleagues and perform career-development research. The virtual revolution breaks geographic boundaries, which is especially useful for those willing or wanting to relocate.

RESUMÉ DATABASES

The computer effortlessly processes ridiculously large amounts of data. That fact, combined with the ability to scan written material accurately, makes massive resumé databases a reality.

These databases contain either full-text resumés, condensed job-seeker profiles or capsule candidate information leading to full resumés. Depending on the service, resumés can be uploaded or e-mailed directly into the system, filled out on-line, or sent to the service via e-mail, fax or in hard copy to be scanned or entered manually by the service's staff.

Rates for enrolling a resumé into a database vary from free to a high of about $75. Resumés usually stay in these databases 6 months to a year; some services have unlimited renewal.

Resumé-database services are used by employers, recruiters, and placement firms. Searches among thousands of resumés in any of these databases are executed either directly on-line by the employer or recruiter or performed by the staff of the database service according to specified parameters.

Work experience, skills, geographic areas, educational and professional degrees, and other attributes and qualifications are specified in targeted key-word searches. Some resumé-database firms charge employers per-search, some per-candidate-identified-by-the-search, and some on a retainer basis (to supply a company with qualified applicants over a specified period of time).

NOT JUST FOR ACTIVE JOB-SEEKERS

A number of resumé-database firms report that most candidates in their databases are employed. Eventually, having one's resumé in such databases may become an accepted fact of work life and not an indication of an active job-hunt. The new reality: jobs are not forever and it's natural for people to make themselves available for new opportunities.

Still, confidentiality can present a problem for those currently employed. Some resumé-database companies address this issue by providing information to the employer only with the candidate's approval. Employers, too, have concerns about confidentiality. Many prefer that their competitors remain unaware of a strategic opening in their ranks.

WHAT ARE MY CHANCES?

The high ratio of resumés to job opportunities lessens the likelihood of landing your dream job—even if you're in one or more resumé databases. But exposure does create potential which is why these services are growing.

Resumé databases are building so rapidly that some services are having difficulty updating their systems quickly enough to keep pace. This seems to lower the chances for any individual job-seeker's resumé to be pulled in a search. But take heart. Based on the diverse job functions and industries that are represented, more employers will use the services to find candidates.

KNOW YOUR TARGETS

It's important to understand the methodology of each resumé database service you choose. The best services will help you tailor your resumé (profile, skills, qualifications, experience, etc.) to the form and language their computer search will recognize.

For example, many resumé experts advise using action verbs to describe abilities, but many resumé-scanning and key-word-search systems use nouns. Sometimes even the kind of paper the resumé is on can affect the process. A complete discussion on how to prepare an effective scannable resumé appears on page 28.

If you're uploading your resumé on-line rather than sending a resumé to be scanned, be aware that on most systems your information will be stripped of any fancy fonts, bold, or italics. Rely here on spacing and judicious use of upper and lower case for effective presentation.

The opposite presentation extreme can be found on the graphic-intensive World Wide Web portion of the Internet. Here "uploaded" resumés (in HTML format) can appear with pictures, photographs, even audio and video clips, in addition to distinctive, carefully laid-out text.

Savvy job-hunters learn these and other tactics to maximize their visibility in candidate databases. Be creative: Think of clever ways to position yourself. If you seek to relocate, find databases that specialize geographically. This field is full of niches to be explored once you've targeted your search.

JOB POSTINGS ON-LINE

Computer listings of job openings are the logical flipside to resumé databases. On-line job postings can be searched by function, industry, location or a combination of these parameters.

Some services charge the employer or recruiter/placement firm that places the "ad." A few recruiting services and major companies have even developed their own service for their own listings. Others charge the job-seeker who searches the listings. Still others charge both!

Posting time limits (renewable upon request) keeps most information current. There are occasional complaints by users about "stale" listings. But employers, who don't want to be inundated with responses to already-filled positions, are also motivated to keep their postings current.

Accessing on-line job postings is a proactive practice. Listings change frequently; services have their own niches. Novices should try services with local phone access to practice maneuvering on-line without the on-the-meter pressure of a long-distance phone call. You'll also get valuable experience in using your communications software's screen-capturing feature (which saves a "snapshot" view of the information on your screen for review later). It can save you a lot of money. Local bulletin boards, state employment offices and the services of local libraries are good places to start.

Response to an on-line job opportunity can be by mail, phone, fax or, increasingly, on-line.

The job-seeker who participates in this high-tech recruitment method automatically demonstrates skills now considered significant in most workplaces. Employers receiving responses to on-line job openings are virtually guaranteed applicants with a "prescreened" working knowledge of computers. Having your own e-mail address can greatly facilitate networking, which is still critically important for job-seekers.

Until recently, the vast majority of jobs listed on-line have been technically oriented. On-line job postings are still rife with computer programmer/MIS/engineering positions. This is to be expected not only because of the target audience, but also because technical skills are relatively easy to label and categorize.

But the nature and number of on-line job listings is rapidly broadening as computer and modem use sweeps the business landscape. Not only are all kinds of jobs posted, but the modem allows employers to literally scan the world for people with exactly the right credentials.

Employers actually report a higher percentage of highly qualified candidates (50 percent) responding to on-line job postings as opposed to the 10 to 15 percent garnered through traditional print advertising.

One of the most active parts of the job-posting field involves improving access to help-wanted ads. A growing company called Classifacts, for example, gathers Sunday help-wanted ads from 40 newspapers throughout the country. Job-seekers call in and request a search on specific job titles (performed by the Classifacts staff), and can purchase the results (deliverable by mail or fax). Classifacts may become available on the Internet. Watch for other services like it.

But what of positions, often high-level, that would never be advertised? Not surprisingly, on-line job-posting services and resumé-database services report growing use by executive recruiters using them as a means for identifying potential candidates (sourcing).

While executive search will remain a largely personalized and confidential process, recruiters are finding that posting jobs on-line produces sources and candidates quickly and economically. It is an appropriate outlet for at least some of their assignments.

OTHER ON-LINE OPTIONS

A number of on-line employment services work on both sides of the matchmaking equation. Many post job openings *and* maintain a resumé database.

Often these services include downloadable files (mostly shareware) relating to employment and career issues—everything from resumé-preparation software to career-planning and interview exercises. Message areas, sometimes moderated by professional career counselors, offer a forum for job-seekers to exchange experiences and tips. Ideally the networking that evolves from communicating this way can lead to employment.

Professional associations are increasingly involved in offering on-line job search/ resumé database services as a membership benefit. Some have allied with existing on-line job-and-career service businesses, while others are managing their own systems.

All major on-line services offer some form of job-and-career information, either in a broad subject area or a specialty subgroup. Some services carry job listings or accept resumés for other private services.

There are more than 60,000 local bulletin boards in the U.S., and 40,000 more worldwide. Many of these are linked through bulletin board system (bbs) networks. Some of these homegrown networks, particularly FIDONet and JOBNet, carry job postings, and resumé database/jobs wanted listings. Information entered via a local bbs is "echoed" (shared) on the many participating bulletin board systems across the country.

THE INTERNET

Then, of course, there is the Internet—the fastest-growing international on-line information system of all. The Internet is quickly evolving into on-line's most important general business tool. In response to the Internet's mushrooming appeal, all of the major on-line services are scrambling to provide access (particularly to the World Wide Web).

Universities, traditionally the bastion of Internet access, post their own job openings and those of related research institutions. University alumni associations have also become active in on-line job services, including resumé databases for experienced alums as well as entry-level graduates.

One of the largest and most popular private job-and-career resource accessed via the Internet is the Online Career Center (OCC). The nonprofit OCC, supported by more than 200 member companies, provides job-and-career information, company profiles, job listings, a resumé database, and access to other Internet-based job-and-career resources. The OCC reports a resumé database of nearly 20,000 names (free entry), growing by 160 a day, and a listing of up to 12,000 jobs. The OCC tallies more than 4 million individual visits per month. Workers and employers in the U.S., Japan, England, France, and Germany are the biggest users of this system.

Internet career resources—resumé databases, job posting locations, career management resources—are now opening up on the Internet faster than can be catalogued. Many employers package job postings with other profile information or link the postings to their World Wide Web home page. Newspapers, associations, recruiters, and individuals are flocking to the Internet to prospect for jobs or clients or to sell their wares.

GOVERNMENT INFORMATION

The U.S. Government, spurred by the current pro "information highway" administration, uses on-line technology to help inform its citizenry. Federal job-and-career information is provided on-line through a series of agencies. The government has also embraced this technology as part of its military-to-civilian transition planning.

Government and industry are involved in preparations to create one-stop career centers. Here, public access to vast databases of occupational information will be sorted and delivered electronically as an aid to individual career planning. State governments, too, are currently enlisting on-line technology.

RESEARCHING YOUR TARGET COMPANY

Another opportunity on the on-line highway is for employment-related research: identifying organizations you might like to join, and finding out everything about them.

Here again, all major on-line services and many smaller specialized services offer resources to help you. Using these services, you could:

- Identify firms in an industry specialty within a specific geographic area
- Electronically sort and create mailing lists and labels for companies or recruiters that fit an area of interest or expertise
- Learn more about organizations to enhance interview performance

Many of these services are complex, expensive, and aimed at the professional researcher, so hiring a pro to help is prudent in some instances. Innovative outplacement firms have also included on-line research in their repertoire of career planning/job search techniques. Here again, the burgeoning Internet provides rich deposits of research information just waiting to be mined. The hypertext feature of the World Wide Web often accomplishes much of the task by linking scattered resources together.

Every day more reference texts, directories, and other collections of business information are appearing in electronic (i.e. searchable, selectively printable) form, either as CD-ROM products or as a component of an on-line research service. Libraries play a central role in these new forms of information dissemination, and are now frequented by white-collar job-seekers performing business research.

DO ON-LINE SERVICES WORK?

Success rates for on-line job search and resumé databases are difficult to determine. That's because the businesses that maintain these services normally don't go beyond the employer/potential employee "handshake."

These firms are not employment brokers or placement agencies; they only match and introduce. Job-seekers express confidence in this method by renewing their resumé placements in resumé databases.

In what must be a reflection (or at least a perception) of effectiveness, companies large and small are subscribing to and supporting on-line recruiting methods. But as outplacement firms, career counselors, and veteran job-seekers will all verify, finding a new job requires a multi-faceted, proactive approach using every available resource. Searching on-line job postings and placing resumés in resumé databases are potent high-tech tools that can augment the process.

TECHNICAL QUESTIONS

The use of modems and on-line services does take some getting used to and, as with many new tools, there's no substitute for experience. For the home user, though, certain words and FAQs (on-line lingo for Frequently Asked Questions) pop up over and over. Without getting too technical, here are some common settings and tips for functioning smoothly on-line.

What *Is* a Modem?

A modem transmits and receives computer data over a telephone line (the word *modem* is short for modulate/demodulate). Modems can be internal (mounted inside your computer) or external models. Both function the same way. Modems are rated in bps or baud.

What Are BPS and Baud?

Bps (bits per second) and baud are sometimes used interchangeably although they are not the same. What's important to know is that bps and baud relate to the speed at which a modem handles and transfers data. The trick with bps is that it takes both modems (the system you've logged onto, and your system) to create the rate. The higher the bps rate the faster the data will flow. Typical bps rates (higher is faster i.e. better) are 300, 600, 1200, 2400, 4800, 9600, 14.4, and now 28.8. Even faster transfer rates can be realized through ISDN technology and perhaps, in the future, through cable interface.

How Should I Set My Communications Software?

Communications software is the program that links your modem and your computer's operating system. Set it (almost always) at 8,N,1, and we'll spare you the explanation.
 Data Bits: 8
 Parity: N
 Stop Bits: 1
 Internet communications software for PCs and MACs work on TCP/IP protocol and require a different set of software to achieve the interface. There are off-the-shelf commercial packages available for ease of configuration.

What Type of Terminal Am I Using?
What Is My Terminal Emulation?

VT100. Again, don't ask, but unless you know something different about your system, this should work.

Do I Want ANSI Graphics? Can I Display ANSI?

Yes, if the communications software on your computer is set for ANSI you will receive graphic, color screens. If you are using the Terminal communications program from within Windows, answer No—Terminal cannot support ANSI graphics. If you are planning frequent on-line sessions, get a communications package other than Terminal. Many full-featured software packages are available. The major on-line services all have easy-to-use graphical interface software available that is designed only for their systems. Check with them when you subscribe.

What Is ASCII?

ASCII (pronounced ASK-ee) stands for American Standard Code for Information Interchange. It usually refers to a stripped-down version of a text file that can be imported and read by most software applications.

What Is a ZIP File?

ZIP refers to a common compression program that is used to reduce the size of large files for storage or quick transfer. Zipped files must be opened up by unzip software in order to use them.

Do I Want to Use a Full-Screen Text Editor?

Yes. Many systems that allow you to enter messages and e-mail will ask this during initial sign-up. A Full-Screen Text Editor lets you look at the whole message you have written, instead of one line at a time, when you want to make changes before saving and sending it.

Do I Want to Use Hot Keys?

Yes. On certain systems, hot keys allow you to type your letter or number menu choice and have the system immediately respond, without having to press enter.

How Should I Set My Download Protocol?

Z modem on your system and Z modem on the on-line system. That is the fastest setting if you choose to download, i.e., move files from the host computer system into your system.

INTERNET WORDS & WAYS

The "Net" has its own peculiar, specific language describing its parts and procedures. The facilities of the Internet can be used for public and private messaging, public relations and advertising, research, file transfer and download. Locations on the Internet—sites—each have unique addresses. Major categories include:

.edu—*educational institutions*
.gov—*government institutions*
.com—*commercial organizations*
.net—*Internet service providers*

E-mail Electronic mail may be the most popular use of the Internet. Messages can be sent through all the major on-line services and the Internet itself, worldwide, in moments. In addition to speeding communications, e-mail can reduce long distance phone bills and paper handling.

E-mail addresses look like: yourname@yourcompany.com. Web addresses are called URLs (Uniform Resource Locators) and may look like this: http:// www.comp.com/. Web browsing software is required to access and view these sites. Gopher, telnet and ftp sites are similar but must be launched through software that supports those formats.

World Wide Web (The Web) An area of the Internet where users can browse documents, called pages, that can contain full color graphics. Pages on the Web can contain hypertext links—addresses of other pages on the Web that can be retrieved by clicking on the address. The Web is the fastest growing area of the Internet and, for many, has finally made the Net accessible for the "non-professional" user.

Gopher A gopher site enables data in text form to be filed, listed and accessed.

Telnet Enables you to log onto another computer from your computer. Some bulletin board services are accessible by telnet.

FTP File transfer protocol is used for downloading files onto your computer from a directory at an Internet site.

IRC Internet Relay Chat allows "live typed conversation" over the Net.

USENET or **Newsgroups** Specialty public messaging boards. Messages can be posted or read on nearly any topic imaginable.

PREPARING A SCANNABLE RESUMÉ

There's a new technology that could help you find your next job. It's called electronic applicant tracking, and it's being used by leading businesses and organizations.

By using the latest in document imaging technology, your resumé can be scanned into a computer system and kept "active" for years. The computer can search for just about anything in your resumé. You could be qualified and considered for jobs you never thought of or knew about. The computer can make it easier for you to be considered for more jobs, and it keeps your resumé on file so it's easier to update your information.

Here's how it works. Your resumé is scanned into the computer as an image. Then OCR (optical character recognition) software looks at the image to distinguish every letter and number (character) and creates a text file (ASCII). Then a program "reads" the text and extracts important information about you such as your name, address, phone number, work history, years of experience, education, and skills.

Why is it important for you to know this? When you prepare a resumé for the computer to read, you want it to be "scannable." A scannable resumé is clean so the scanner can get a clean image. A scannable resumé uses standard fonts and crisp, dark type such as a laser printer or typewriter with a new ribbon would produce—so the OCR can recognize every letter. And a scannable resumé has plenty of facts for the program to extract—the more skills and facts you provide, the more opportunities you'll have for your skills to match available positions.

Preparing a scannable resumé is simple. Like the traditional style resumé, you focus on format and content.

FORMAT

To maximize the computer's ability to read your resumé, provide the cleanest possible original and use a standard style resumé.

The computer can extract skills from many styles of resumés such as chronological, functional, key word (organized by skills rather than job titles), and combinations of resumé types.

The most difficult resumé for the computer to read is a poor quality copy that has an unusual format such as a newsletter layout, adjusted spacing, large font sizes, graphics or lines, type that is too light, or paper that is too dark.

Use the following guidelines to maximize the computer's ability to "read" your resumé:

- Use white or light-colored 8 ½ x 11 paper, printed on one side only.
- Provide a laser printer original if possible. A typewritten original or a high quality photocopy is okay. Avoid dot matrix printouts and low quality copies.
- Do not fold or staple.
- Use standard typefaces such as Helvetica, Futura, Optima, Univers, Times, Palatino, New Century Schoolbook, and Courier.
- Use a font size of 10 to 14 points. (Avoid Times 10 point.)
- Don't condense spacing between letters.
- Use boldface and/or all capital letters for section headings as long as the letters don't touch each other.
- Avoid fancy treatments such as italics, underline, shadows, and reverses (white letters on black background).
- Avoid vertical and horizontal lines, graphics, and boxes.
- Avoid a two-column format or resumés that look like newspapers or newsletters.
- Place your name at the top of the page on its own line. (Your name can also be the first text on pages two and three.)
- Use a standard address format below your name.
- List each phone number on its own line.

CONTENT

The computer extracts information from your resumé. You can use your current resumé. However, once you understand what the computer searches for, you may decide to add a few key words to increase your opportunities for matching requirements or getting "hits."

Recruiters and managers access the resumé database in many ways, searching for your resumé specifically or searching for applicants with specific experience. When searching for specific experience, they'll search for key words, usually nouns such as writer, B.A., marketing collateral, Society of Technical Communication, Spanish (language fluency), San Diego, etc.

So make sure you describe your experience with concrete words rather than vague descriptions. The computer system will extract the words and information from your sentences; you can write your resumé as usual.

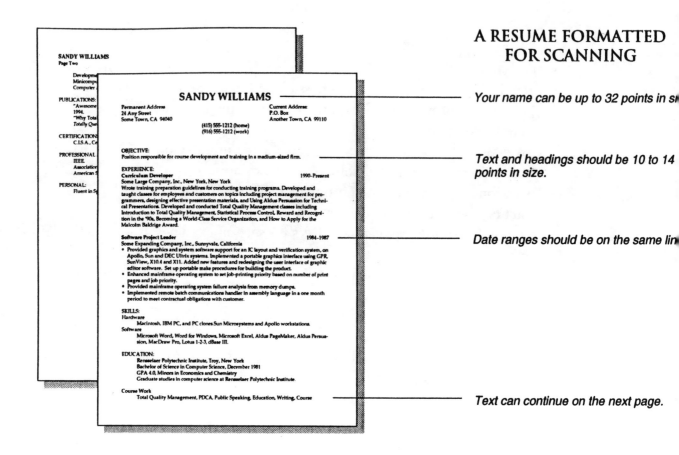

A RESUME FORMATTED FOR SCANNING

Your name can be up to 32 points in si

Text and headings should be 10 to 14 points in size.

Date ranges should be on the same lin

Text can continue on the next page.

TIPS FOR MAXIMIZING "HITS"

Use the following guidelines to maximize your ability to get "hits" (a hit is when one of your skills matches the computer search):

- Use enough key words to define your skills, experience, education, professional affiliations, etc.
- Describe your experience with concrete words rather than vague descriptions. For example, it's better to use "managed a team of software engineers" than "responsible for managing, training . . ."
- Be concise and truthful.
- Use more than one page if necessary. The computer can easily handle multiple-page resumés, and it uses all of the information it extracts from your resumé to determine if your skills match available positions. It allows you to provide more information than you would for a human reader.

- Use jargon and acronyms specific to your industry (spell out the acronyms for human readers).
- Increase your list of key words by including specifics, for example, list the names of software you use such as *Microsoft Word* and *Lotus 1-2-3*.
- Use common headings such as: *Objective, Experience, Employment, Work History, Positions Held, Appointments, Skills, Summary, Summary of Qualifications, Accomplishments, Strengths, Education, Affiliations, Professional Affiliations, Publications, Papers, Licenses, Certifications, Examinations, Honors, Personal, Additional, Miscellaneous, References,* etc.
- If you have extra space, you may wish to describe your personal traits and attitude. Key words could include *skill in time management, dependable, high energy, leadership, sense of responsibility, good memory*.

Additional Considerations

- Some people may want to have two versions of their resumé:

  One for the computer to read—with a scannable format and detailed information. Send this one.

  One for people to read—possibly with a creative layout, enhanced typography, and summarized information. Carry this one to the interview.

- When faxing, set the fax to "fine mode"; the recipient will get a better quality copy.

3
ON-LINE RESOURCE LISTINGS

NOTE: The information in this chapter was accurate and comprehensive at press time, yet this is a rapidly evolving field and medium which defies commitment to print for an extended period of time. The sources listed may have changed phone/fax numbers, prices, and specialties, so you must do some checking on your own.

MAJOR ON-LINE SERVICES

All of the major on-line services offer some form of job-and-career-related information. All of the services also offer different pricing plans which frequently change and may be difficult to compare. Trial memberships allow a good look at the variety of services and relative ease-of-use of these systems. Most new computers now come equipped with modems and are packaged with software and free introductory time on one or more of these services. Magazine ads also often tout trial memberships with free introductory time. Much of the job-and-career information found through these services can be accessed elsewhere but, taken in combination with the broad array or other features that they offer, subscribing to these services can be worthwhile. All of these services offer limited Internet access; most are moving towards full World Wide Web access.

America Online (AOL)
America Online Inc.
8619 Westwood Center Drive
Vienna, VA 22182-2285
800-227-6364, 703-448-8700
FAX 703-883-1509

AOL's Career Center provides a variety of career-management tools and professional guidance including: resumé and cover letter templates, employer contacts database, career information related messaging (also found within several specialty groups), job listings from E-Span JobSearch, Help Wanted USA, and the World Wide Resumé Talent Bank. The Career Center is managed by James Gonyea of Gonyea & Associates, Inc., administrators of Help Wanted USA and the World Wide Resumé Talent Bank.

CompuServe
CompuServe Inc.
5000 Arlington Centre Boulevard
PO Box 20212
Columbus, OH 43220
800-848-8199
FAX 614-457-0348

CompuServe, considered by many to be the most business oriented of the major on-line services, carries E-Span JobSearch listings, has a classifieds area, special interest forums which include networking style discussions, and an extensive database of newspapers, periodicals and research sources.

Delphi
A Service of General Videotex Corporation
Cambridge, MA
800-695-4005, 617-491-3393
FAX 617-491-6642

Perhaps best known for its *full* Internet access, Delphi also has a host of member services including a Job Complex in the Custom Forums section, and classifieds and employment opportunities in the Business Forum area reached through Groups & Clubs. The Job Complex contains conferencing and mail, an Internet gopher, an employment database, an interviewing exercise and more.

GEnie
General Electric Network for Information Exchange
401 North Washington Street
Rockville, MD 20850
800-638-9636

GEnie has an assortment of job and career related information including its Peer-to-Peer Network for specialized industry discussions found in the Health Care Providers

Category, Judge & Lawyers Corner Category, Engineers on GEnie Category and other categories. The Workplace Roundtable section is for general business and employment information, advice, and live conferences, as is the Home Office/Small Business RoundTable. GEnie also carries E-Span JobSearch's open job postings; and Dr. Job, a weekly question and answer column covering career and employment issues written by journalist Sandra Pesmen.

Prodigy
Prodigy Services Company
445 Hamilton Avenue
White Plains, NY 10601
800-776-3449

This fast-growing on-line service carries on-line classifieds and a Careers Bulletin Board for networking with professional colleagues. Prodigy offers an easy-to-use Internet World Wide Web interface.

RESUMÉ DATABASES

American Computerized Employment Service (ACES)
PO Box 27907
Santa Ana, CA 92799-7907
714-250-0221
FAX 714-757-7071

Employee applicants submit Resumé Enrollment Form for ACES to enter data into computer system ($39.95), or submit data on ACES' Resumé Entry program on disk ($19.95 + $3.50 p&h). Fee includes ACES job search guide book with Skills Directory containing over 7,000 job-related skills, and a copy of the resumé after entry to the databank. Employers search the databank by touchtone phone. ACES is going online with The Microsoft Network, expanding nationally. Primary focus is on administrative, professional, and technical positions.

Career Database
PO Box 626
Provincetown, MA 02657
508-487-2238

Charges job seeker $50/annually to input resumé and job description information into its database, over 85% of candidates re-enroll annually. Career Database does not scan resumés, but uses a specially designed profile form. The database is open free of charge to prescreened companies and recruiters. Career Database also offers career counseling and job search assistance.

Career Net Online
1788 Wyrick Avenue
San Jose, CA 95124
800-392-7967
408-269-3910
FAX 408-269-5608

Individual job seeker pays $42 to have profile or "Mini-Resumé" included in a searchable on-line database (50% currently employed). Same profile or "Mini-Resumé" will also be mailed to 3,000 employers and search firms for an additional fee of $53. Service for experienced professional, managerial and executive level (all functions) in United States, Canada and international. Over 20,000 employers/search firms provided with free access to this database.

Career Resumés
PO Box 509
Goldens Bridge, NY 10526
914-232-1412, 800-800-1220
FAX 914-232-8165, 800-927-4611
E-mail: bsjx41a@prodigy.com
http://branch.com/cr/cr.html

Resumé writing company (charges $150–350 to write resumé, free consultation/evaluation). Will post resumé on the Internet for $66/six months.

Corporate Organizing and Research Services (cors)
One Pierce Place
Suite 300 East
Itasca, IL 60143
800-323-1352, 708-250-8677
FAX 708-250-7362

This recruitment research firm has, since 1985, maintained a resumé database of over 1.5 million resumés including all levels and job titles, national and international. Cost is $25 to have resumé entered into database for unlimited time period; no charge for subsequent revisions.

DC's Site for On-line Resumés
John Paul Mains
InterMarket Associates
3902 Penderview Dr. 1401
Fairfax, VA 22033
E-mail: jmains@intr.net
http://www.intr.net/dc-online/resume/

Charges to post resumé on this new Internet World Wide Web site—$30/six months ($5 for changes). Will add links to a resumé already on-line for $10/six month period.

EMPLOYNET
80 Wall Street
Suite 415
New York, NY 10005
212-425-6679
FAX 212-425-4862

Service scans resumés into database ($50 fee/1 year) searched online by recruiters. High level jobs, primarily Northeast, expanding nationwide.

HispanData
360 South Hope Avenue
Suite 300c
Santa Barbara, CA 93105
805-682-5843
FAX 805-687-4546

This resumé database, created to respond to the need for bilingual capabilities, a diverse work force, and the passage of NAFTA contains 15,000 resumés of Hispanic professionals including new college grads and senior executives. The majority are skilled professionals with 3–5 plus years of work experience in sales, marketing, management, accounting, finance, human resources, systems management/ engineering and computer science. Cost is $25 for lifetime enrollment to have resumé online. HispanData is slated to be on the Internet by the end of '95.

IntelliMatch
2107 North First Street
Suite 460
San Jose, CA 95131
408-441-1947
FAX 408-441-7048
E-mail: intelli@netcom.com
http://www.mmasters.com/mmasters/team/watson/index.html
http://www.batnet.com/intellimatch/

Database-matching service uses proprietary Windows PC software named WATSON (Where Applicants Turn Skills into Opportunities Nationwide) to create "structured resumés" that interface with HOLMES (Hiring through On-line Match of Employment Specifications) software used by the searching employers. Postings are in the areas of hardware engineering, software development, marketing, sales, MIS, accounting and finance.

Job Bank USA
1420 Spring Hill Road
Suite 480
McLean, VA 22102
800-296-1872, 703-847-1706
FAX 703-847-1494

This 25,000+ resumé database includes all technical and professional fields at all skill and management levels in all industries, nationwide. A wide range of professional/ technical associations, academic institutions, professional and vocational training institutes and outplacement firms endorse and/or support the Job Bank USA program including: Society for Human Resource Management, National Society for Professional Engineers, American College of Health Care Administrators, American Bar Association, American Production and Inventory Control Society, American Institute of Certified Public Accountants, National Society for Performance & Instruction, and the Alumni Associations of Penn State, Florida State, and the universities of Nebraska, California (Northridge), Texas (Arlington), Delaware, New Mexico, Arkansas, Maryland and Wyoming. Individual fills out enrollment form which, with his or her resumé, is scanned into the database. Cost is $125 for 1 year enrollment and a Career Fitness Kit of books, software, a discount card, catalog, newsletter and other resources for effective job search and career management in the 1990's. 65% of the database is currently employed. Job Bank USA has more than 2,000 active employers requesting searches.

National Employee Database
418 Ashmun Street
Sault Ste. Marie, MI 49783-1906
800-366-3633
FAX 906-632-4495
modem 906-632-3285
E-mail: FONENED@aol.com

National database containing over 15,000 resumés offered directly on-line to 750+ employers and recruiters through subscription. Job seekers (75–80% are degreed professionals earning $50,000 plus) send resumé and $25 for a 1-year listing of their resumé on-line. Hard copy resumés are scanned for employer fax-back capability. Resumés may also be transmitted electronically via Internet e-mail. Recruiters, placement companies, and employers (45% recruiters) subscribe for 3 months for $120 plus pay for access time at $3.60/hour.

National Resumé Bank
3637 Fourth Street North
Suite 330
St. Petersburg, FL 33704
813-896-3694
FAX 813-894-1277
modem 813-822-7082

National employment database of approx. 4,500 candidates. 600 prescreened employers access the resumé bank for free. Candidates range from clerical to CEO, with salary levels from mid $20,000 to $100,000 plus. Candidate pays $40 for an unlimited listing in one category, $10 charge for each additional category, fills out a 50-word qualification summary (arranged in keyword format) and supplies five hard copy resumés. Job categories are: Advertising/Public Relations, Aerospace, Airlines, Architecture, Clerical, Communications, Computers/Data Processing, Creative, Distribution, Education, Engineering, Entertainment, Environmental, Financial, General, Government, Health Care, Hospitality, Human Resources, Insurance, International Business, Law Enforcement, Legal, Management, Manufacturing, Marketing, Medical, Purchasing, Real Estate, Research, Retail, Sales, Social Sciences, Technical, Trades. National Resumé Bank, founded in 1992, is a service of The Professional Association of Resumé Writers whose members can enter job candidates into the database.

Online Resumé Service (see Online Career Center)
1713 Hemlock Lane
Plainfield, IN 46168

For those who have no e-mail access, the Online Resumé Service will, for $10, place a resumé into the Online Career Center resumé database for 6 months.

Placement Services Ltd.
265 South Main Street
Akron, Ohio 44308
216-762-0279
FAX 216-762-7031

There is no charge to include a resumé in this resumé databank. The resumé database is primarily drawn from magazines including Datamation, EDN, Industrial Engineering, Design News, Society Petroleum Engineers International, Clean Rooms, JPT and other sources. Executive recruiters, management consultants and companies pay a fee per candidate identified in a search.

Recruiters OnLine Network
http://www.onramp.net/ron

Online association of recruiters, employment agencies, search firms and employment professionals provides tools and resources for professionals and has a resumé-posting service for job-seekers. Resumé database is searchable by member firms.

The Resumé File
Simi Valley, CA
modem 805-581-6210

Employment-oriented fee-based service (no charge for limited access) has listings of nationwide openings and a resumé database for all functions and industries. Includes many nationwide job network conferences and extensive downloadable file resource area.

Resumé Link
3972 C Brown Park Drive
PO Box 218
Hilliard, Ohio 43026
614-777-4000
FAX 614-771-5708

This company maintains a resumé database for 15 professional associations including eight engineering societies: The American Society of Mechanical Engineers, The Society of Manufacturing Engineers, The Society of Automotive Engineers, The American Ceramic Society, ASM International, IEEE, Society of Plastics Engineers, and The Society of Women Engineers. Resumé Link also manages the 20,000 entry National Resumé Database of Computer & Engineering Professionals and creates, produces and distributes customized resumé database systems to MBA programs in the U.S. and Europe, universities, newspapers, outplacement firms, corporations, government agencies, and job and career fairs. Candidates stay in database for 1 year, service is a membership benefit.

Shawn's Internet Resumé Center
NovaNet, Inc.
2007 N. 15 Street, Suite 5
Arlington, VA 22201
703-524-4800
FAX 703-534-5033
E-mail: shawn@novanet.com
http://www.nsbc.com/sirc/resmectr.html

Charges $15 setup and $15 per three months to post resumé on the Internet. Offering other services to job-seekers including those of a professional resumé writing company called Just Your Type.

SkillSearch
104 Woodmont Boulevard
Suite 306
Nashville, Tennessee 37205
800-258-6641
FAX 615-834-9453

Database of white collar professionals (4 yr. degree and min. 2 years work experience) recruited primarily through 60 university alumni associations. Costs $65 for 2 year listing, $15 annual renewal fee. Over 99% of almost 40,000 database currently employed ($250,000 highest salary, most $50–60,000). Many technical, engineering, MIS, scientific, and MBAs. Will prepare resumé for member.

Technology Registry
616 Carolina Street
San Francisco, CA 94107
415-641-3838
FAX 415-641-3188
http://www.techreg.com/techreg/

Designed as a recruiting tool, TR includes resumés in its database of individuals and organizations in the technology industries. Also maintains Web site with easy resumé form.

University ProNet
2445 Faber Place, Suite 200
Palo Alto, CA 94303
800-726-0280, 415-845-4000
FAX 415-845-4019

Resumé database service (lifetime registration available) for alumni of member universities only, accessed by a multitude of companies nationwide. Universities participating include: University of California at Berkeley, and at L.A., CalTech, Carnegie Mellon, University of Chicago, University of Michigan, University of Pennsylvania, Columbia, Cornell, MIT, Stanford, Yale and others. (Contact your alumni association for membership information.) $25 fee gives active job seekers database listing and Job Bulletin for six months.

Walt Disney Productions
E-mail: resumes@disney.com

There is no fee required to upload resumés via e-mail to be considered for technical, computer science, and software positions. (The Disney Applicant Information System, DAISY, has been discontinued.)

World Job Seekers
http://cban.worldgate.edmonton.ab.ca/resume/index.html

New, free Internet resumé posting service contains names of people from around the world (strongly Canadian oriented) who are seeking employment.

World Wide Resumé/Talent Bank
Gonyea & Associates, Inc.
3543 Enterprise Road East
Safety Harbor, Florida 34695
813-725-9600
America Online: careerdoc
E-mail: careerdoc@aol.com
http://www.webcom.com/~career/hwusa.html

An extensive resumé database for job seekers and consultants. $40 enters a resumé listing for 1 year. Currently contains over 12,000 resumés.

JOB POSTINGS ON-LINE

Access...FCO On-Line
Federal Research Service, Inc.
243 Church Street, NW
PO Box 1059
Vienna, VA 22183-1059
703-281-0200
FAX 703-281-7639

This private company provides a computerized version of the Federal Career Opportunities bi-weekly publication listing entry level to senior executive, national and overseas federal jobs. Individuals pay $45 for one hour of access time (good for a 1-year period) plus a $25 initial setup fee.

Andersen Consulting
http://www.ac.com/recruit/workn.htm

Job postings and info on large international management consulting company.

Career Link Worldwide
PO Box 11720
Phoenix, AZ 85061
voice 602-841-2134
FAX 602-841-5981
modem 602-973-2002

Since 1984, posts jobs—US & overseas—everything from trades on up to high executive level. Gets its listings from companies, recruiters and publications. Job seekers pay to access the service on-line: $15/month + .15/min @1200 bps, .30/min. @2400 bps; 9600 & 14,400 bps available Career Link Worldwide maintains 1,300 new jobs categorized by career field.

Career Magazine
http://www.careermag.com/careermag

Produced by NCS Jobline of Boulder, Colorado, this on-line magazine is free to job seekers and human resource professionals. The Web site includes job postings, and a wide variety of career resources and employer profile information. Management, accounting, sales and marketing job postings can be retrieved by searching occupational titles, skills and geographic locations.

Career Mosaic
Bernard Hodes Advertising, Inc.
555 Madison Avenue
New York, NY 10022
800-624-7744, 212-758-2600
FAX 212-759-5781, 212-753-1106
E-mail: tgibbon@hodes.com
http://www.careermosaic.com/cm/home.html

This Internet World Wide Web server, using cutting edge technology, offers an "electronic careers brochure" on-line. Companies profile their corporate philosophy, products, services, annual reports, financial data and sites in addition to posting job openings and recruiting talent. Career Mosaic incorporates full color graphics, utilizes hypertext capability, and features a searchable jobs database. It provides an excellent location for career management research. Career Mosaic may also be reached through the Online Career Center.

Career Taxi
http://www.iquest.net/Career—Taxi/taxi.html

Graphic-intensive Web site features job postings, career advice, company information.

careerWEB
150 West Brambleton Avenue
Norfolk, VA 23510
804-446-2900, 800-871-0800
FAX 804-627-2175
E-mail: info@cweb.com
http://www.cweb.com

"Full service career site" provides searchable job postings, employer profiles, career fair and franchise opportunity info for job seekers.

Chicago Tribune Classifieds
E-mail: webmaster@tribune.com
http://www.chicago.tribune.com/

Help wanted ads in five technical categories, feature articles about employment and employers.

FEDERAL GOVERNMENT JOB OPENINGS

There are several ways to view postings of Federal government job openings. Some of the same listings appear in more than one location, on more than one bulletin board system. Dartmouth College also gathers and posts federal job openings. (Internet: gopher.dartmouth.edu, Dartmouth College, Career Services, Job Openings in the Federal Government.) Supplementary materials at Dartmouth's site include Salary Pay Tables for Federal Civilian Employees; Locality Pay Tables for Federal Employees; Federal Job Classification Information; and Federal Group Occupational Requirements. The service also has: national and international job postings (mostly high tech) from the private sector and contact information for individual state government employment offices.

FedWorld
FedWorld, run by the National Technical Information Service (NTIS), is a gateway connection to many, many federal bulletin board systems and can be highly informative about many aspects of federal government operations.
Internet: telnet fedworld.doc.gov
http://www.fedworld.gov
ftp.fedworld.gov
modem 703-321-8020

Choose menu option (J) Federal Job Openings.

Federal Job Opportunity Board
Office of Personnel Management
Staffing Service Center
4685 Log Cabin Drive
Macon, GA 31298
voice 912-757-3030
modem 912-757-3100
Internet: telnet fjob.mail.opm.gov (198.78.46.10)

Complete list of federal job vacancies by region and state. Text and ZIP (compressed) files are available for download.

Federal Job Info Center: FJOB BBS
modem 912-757-3100
voice 313-226-4423
Federal job listings and information for all U.S.

Federal Jobline
May be accessed through regional offices of the Office of Personnel Management:
Atlanta, GA
voice 404-331-3459
modem 404-730-2370
Dallas, TX
voice 214-767-8245
modem 214-767-0565, 214-767-5471
Detroit, MI
voice 313-226-6950
modem 313-226-4423
Los Angeles, CA
modem 818-575-6521
Philadelphia, PA
modem 215-580-2216

Federal Government LISTSERV
Postings of Federal Job Openings.
Address: fedjobs@dartcms1.dartmouth.edu
Subscribe to: LISTSERV@dartcms1.dartmouth.edu
From: <your address>
Subject: (leave blank)
Message: Subscribe fedjobs <firstname> <lastname>

CapAccess Career Center
The National Capital Area Public Access Network, Inc.
Washington, DC
modem 202-785-1523
Internet: Telnet to cap.gwu.edu

Job info for the National Institutes of Health, National Science Foundation, Federal Gov, and more. No fee required. Login: GUEST, password: VISITOR, type "go careers".

Department of Commerce
modem 301-763-4574
voice 301-763-5780

Posts Census Bureau employment opportunities.

Department of Defense
news:dod.jobs

Newsgroup for posting job announcements from the U.S. Department of Defense.

Department of the Interior
modem 800-368-3321

AVADS-BBS, The Automated Vacancy Announcement Information Center posts permanent and part-time positions available with the Department of the Interior.

Department of Justice
Internet: gopher.usdoj.gov
gopher://justice2.usdoj.gov/1/jobs

Job listings for attorneys, positions with the various offices of the Inspector General.

Department of Labor
modem 212-219-4784

Downloadable files of federal job opportunities nationwide.

GETAJOB!!!
http://www.teleport.com/~pcllgn/gaj.html

Free service to job-seekers (charges employers and other advertisers) offers a wide array of posted job openings as well as links to business' home pages, other job placement and recruiting services.

helpwanted.com
Your Software Solutions, Inc.
771 Boston Post Road, #182
Marlborough, MA 01752
508 485-1230
FAX 508 481-9616
E-mail: editor@helpwanted.com
gopher.helpwanted.com

Gopher server on the Internet posts mostly Boston metro area jobs in computers, engineering, programming, management and finance.

Help Wanted - USA
Gonyea & Associates, Inc.
3543 Enterprise Road East
Safety Harbor, Florida 34695
813-725-9600
America Online: careerdoc
Internet: careerdoc@aol.com
http://www.webcom.com/~career/hwusa.html

A database of employment information and listings gathered from employers, recruiters, state employment agencies, career planning centers, job bbs's, local newspapers and classified ads (more than 60 people collect information in their local areas). Has 5–6,000 professional level listings. Charges $75/ad for 2 week listing.

The Lynn Borne Employment Network
6934 Canby Avenue #109
Reseda, CA 91335
818-881-9353
FAX 818-881-2796
modem 310-445-0633, 310-372-4050, 213-936-1160, 818-557-2131
type GO LBNET

International, national & southern California middle and upper level accounting, finance, marketing & manufacturing job listings posted by an affiliation of executive search firms.

Millkern Communications Gopher
Internet: gopher millkern.com

Lists state government listings, has pointers to Federal Government listings, university jobs and the Online Career Center.

National Physician Job Listings Directory
http://www.njnet.com/~embbs/job/jobs.html

Lists practice opportunities throughout North America for all medical specialties.
The Nonprofit/Fundraising JobNet
Philanthropy Journal of North Carolina
http://www.nando.net/philant

North Carolina area listings of job openings at nonprofits (development officer, account manager, etc.).

STATE GOVERNMENTS

Many states are maintaining computerized job posting databases, but most can only be accessed at the state divisions of employment security (call your local branch). A national job bank of hard to fill positions, The Automated Labor Exchange (ALEX) system, originates in Albany, New York. Postings from the ALEX system are available on some state systems.

America's Job Bank
http://www.ajb.dni.us/
telnet ajb.dni.us

Joint effort of the 2000 offices of the State Employment Service. Newly created service already posting over 100,000 public and private sector jobs; listings are compiled by the U.S. Department of Labor.

Greater Columbus Freenet
Columbus, Ohio
gopher.freenet.columbus.oh.us

Listing of jobs available within the state of Ohio.

Indiana
Indiana State Department of Personnel
http://source.isd.state.in.us/acin/personnel/

Listings of jobs available with the state of Indiana.

Maine
State of Maine
Bureau of Human Resources
State Office Building, Room 214
State House Station #4
Augusta, Maine 04333-0004
207-287-3761
FAX 207-287-4563
http://www.state.me.us/bhr/career.htm

Listing of career opportunities in Maine State Government.

Montana Job Service
http://JSD_Server.DLI.MT.GOV

"Self Directed Job Search System" provided by the Montana Job Service. System contains listings of job openings located in Montana searchable by selecting an occupational category and geographical location. Includes complete listing of Montana Job Service offices.

Nebraska Online
Omaha, NE
800-392-7932

State of Nebraska state job listings and other state related info. No fee required.

North Carolina
http://www.esc.state.nc.us

Access to the North Carolina Employment Security Commission's database of job listings and labor market info. An average of 50,000 clerical to professional level job openings are posted monthly.

Texas Window on State Government
Austin, TX
Window on State Gov 800-227-8392 (in state),
Direct at 512-475-4893, 512-475-3689
Internet: Telnet to window.texas.gov

Contains ALEX and Governors Job Bank which lists all positions available with the state government or government related agencies. Also connects to TEC hi-TEC BBS (Texas Employment Commission) and TEC-HR BBS (Texas Education Agency).

Vermont
Department of Employment
http://www.cit.state.vt.us/det/dethp.

Posts full and part-time job listings organized by geographic region and function/ industry. Includes many other employment resources.

The Virginian-Pilot
http://www.infi.net/pilot/classmain.html

Pilot Online classified ads (help wanted) are updated by 8 p.m. the night before publication in the printed Virginian-Pilot.

SERVICES WITH RESUMÉ DATABASES & JOB POSTINGS

Career Connections
5150 El Camino Real
Suite D33
Los Altos, CA 94022
voice 415-903-5800
FAX 415-903-5848
modem 415-903-5840 (2400 bps), 415-903-5815 (9600-14.4 bps)
E-mail: postmaster@career.com
Internet:
   telnet://career.com for professional listings
   telnet://college.career.com for new college graduate listings
   telnet://jobfair.career.com for CyberFairs
   (virtual job fairs for companies)
World Wide Web: http://www.career.com

Sophisticated menu-driven, interactive recruitment network named H.E.A.R.T.: Human resources Electronic Advertising & Recruiting Tool. No charge for candidates to fill in a profile on-line (the system generates the resumé itself and creates a private password/e-mail/profile account) and access 1500–2000 international job listings. Companies pay to advertise their open positions, mainly professional and managerial jobs. This is a fast-growing system taking full advantage of the latest technology. Career Connections is receiving 580–1,000 resumés/day adding to 69,000 candidates entered since its start in December of '93 on the telnet site and 4500–5500 requests a day on the Web site to view and respond to positions.

Employment Connection
Leominster, MA
modem 508-537-1862

Free service lists positions available at MIT and in Boston area; also has resumé database.

Employment Transition Services Group
888 17th Street NW, 12th Floor
Washington, DC 20036
202-667-3874
FAX: 202-667-7055
E-mail: etsg@idl.com
http://idl.com/etsg/

Employment Transition Services Group (ETSG) uses the Internet to provide outplacement, resumé databases, job postings, consulting, and other services to individuals and public and private sector organizations.

E-Span JobSearch
8440 Woodfield Crossing
Suite 170
Indianapolis, Indiana 46240
800-682-2901, 317-469-4535
FAX 317-469-4508
E-mail: info@espan3.espan.com
E-mail resumé: resumes@espan1.espan.com
http://www.espan.com

Job postings and resumé database accessed through the Internet, America Online, CompuServe, Exec PC, GEnie, e World and specialized bulletin board systems. Through this distribution method, E-Span reaches an audience of 28 million. E-Span JobSearch has over 1,500 jobs listed, mostly technical, also higher level, national and some international which display for a four week standard run time. The database is updated twice a week. Categories include DP/IS, engineering, manufacturing, government, sciences, finance and accounting, education, human resources, medical, pharmaceutical and more. Job seekers can e-mail their resumé for free 6 month entry into a 3,000+ resumé database (growing quickly since the enrollment fee was recently eliminated). E-Span recently launched the Interactive Employment Network (IEN) accessible through the World Wide Web on the Internet to provide a searchable database of over 3,000 high tech job openings and a variety of career management resources. The Web service receives more than 30,000 requests for info each day.

DORS (Defense Outplacement Referral System)
Transition Bulletin Board
Operation Transition
DMDC
DoD Center-Monterey Bay
400 Gigling Road
Seaside, CA 93955-6771
408-655-0400
800-727-3677
FAX 408-656-2132, 408-656-2087

DORS database contains more than 10,000 resumés, and was designed to provide employers with access to Department of Defense members (and their spouses) leaving the armed forces. Signing up with the DORS database is free to service personnel, their spouses and employers. Registered employers have free access to these resumés through DORS, and are encouraged to list job openings, free of charge, on the Transition Bulletin Board.

The Job Board
E-mail: jwsmith@io.org.
http://www.io.org/~jwsmith/jobs.html

Job postings and resumés on an Internet World Wide Web site.

Internet Newsgroups
Many job and career services may be accessed through the expansive Internet, including a variety of employment related newsgroups. Some are very active others have limited traffic. A number of these groups are also posted on and accessed through other services.
alt.medical.sales.jobs.offered
alt.medical.sales.jobs.resumes
at.jobs - Jobs in Austria
atl.jobs - Atlanta employment
austin.jobs - Austin, TX jobs
aus.ads.jobs - Australia jobs open/wanted
ba.jobs.offered - San Francisco Bay Area employment

balt.jobs - Baltimore/Washington DC area jobs
bionet.jobs - Scientific employment
biz.jobs.offered - Business employment
can.jobs - Canadian employment
chi.jobs - Chicago area employment
cle.jobs - Cleveland job postings
dc.jobs - Washington DC employment
de.markt.jobs - Jobs in Germany
dk.jobs - Denmark jobs
dod.jobs - Department of Defense job postings
fl.jobs - Florida jobs
fr.jobs.offers - Jobs offered in France
houston.jobs.offered - Jobs in Houston
ia.jobs - Jobs in Iowa
ie.jobs - Jobs in Ireland
iijnet.jobs - Job openings in Japan.
il.jobs.offered - Illinois area jobs
in.jobs - Jobs in Indiana
la.jobs - Jobs in Los Angeles
mi.jobs - Michigan employment
milw.jobs - Milwaukee employment
misc.jobs.entrylevel - Worldwide
misc.jobs.contract - Worldwide
misc.jobs.offered - Worldwide
ne.jobs - New England employment
relcom.commerce.jobs - Job postings in Russia/Eastern Europe
sdnet.jobs - San Diego jobs
seattle jobs.offered - Jobs in Seattle
stl.jobs - St. Louis employment
swnet.jobs - Jobs in Sweden
triangle.jobs - Triangle Area employment
tx.jobs - Texas employment
uk.jobs.offered - UK employment
us.jobs.contract - United States
us.jobs.offered.entry - United States
us.jobs.offered - United States
za.ads.jobs - jobs in South Africa

Resumés can be uploaded onto the Internet; read the "welcome" posting for each newsgroup for the guidelines on how to post.

atl.resumes
bionet.jobs.wanted
il.jobs.resumes
misc.jobs.misc
misc.jobs.resume
us.jobs.resumes

Lockheed Martin Energy Systems
Oak Ridge, TN
gopher gopher1.ctd.ornl.gov
http://www.ornl.gov/employment.html

Listing of available jobs at Oak Ridge National Laboratory.

MedSearch America, Inc.
15254 NE 95th Street
Redmond, WA 98052
206-883-7252
FAX 206-883-7465
E-mail: office@medsearch.com
gopher.medsearch.com 9001
http://www.medsearch.com:9001

Comprehensive job posting and resumé database service for healthcare professionals nationwide. Covers healthcare positions at all levels. Also has online Healthcareer forums, online healthcare employment articles, industry outlooks and more. No fee for access by job seeker.

The Monster Board
http://www.monster.com

The Monster Board, run by advertising/recruiting firm ADION Information Services, includes over 500 position listings from more than 70 companies. Most of the jobs are on the east coast (primarily New England) in the computing field, but marketing, communications, and other positions are posted as well. Searching can be done by company name, location, discipline, industry and specific job title. Resumés can be entered on an on-line form.

New Hampshire Works
voice 800-852-3400

Online resumé database and job listings available free of charge within state, accessible from home pc, at state employment offices, many libraries, universities and career centers. Resumés stay in for 90 days, job orders for 45 days. New Hampshire Works now has over 2000 resumés, over 1,000 job orders at all levels and searchable by occupation classification, geographic preference or both.

Online Career Center (OCC)
3125 Dandy Trail
Suite 3
Indianapolis, IN 46214
317-293-6499
FAX 317-293-6692
Internet: gopher.occ.com
http://www.occ.com/occ/
E-mail resumé to: occ-resumes@occ.com.

The nonprofit Online Career Center contains searchable job postings (by job title, keyword, company name or geographic region) from over 200 member companies, employment and career information (Career Assistance), and a searchable database of resumés of job seekers. It is designed exclusively for professional, technical and managerial jobs—10–12,000 jobs are currently listed. Resumés can be entered for free—18–20,000 resumés are on the system now; the resumé database can be searched at no charge by any employer with Internet access. Resumés stay on the system for 3 months and, if renewed, can be on indefinitely. For those that cannot e-mail, the Online Resumé Service will place a resumé on the OCC for $10. The Online Career Center is the Internet's first (and most frequently accessed) employment and career database. The popular OCC is one of the fastest growing services available to the users of the Internet as well as subscribers to Prodigy, America Online, CompuServe, Delphi and other commercial networks. The OCC is logging more than 4 million searches per month.

Online Opportunities
422 W. Lincoln Highway, Suite 124
Exton, PA 19341
voice 610-873-6811
Job seeker 24 hour voicemail 610-873-2168
FAX 610-873-4022
E-mail: info@jobnet.com
modem 610-873-7170
Telnet: jobnet.com
WWW: www.jobnet.com

This company runs a BBS which posts positions in the greater Philadelphia area (PRO Job Network) and also carries national Internet, Help Wanted-USA, and E-Span listings. Its resumé database (90% professional level with 5+ years experience) is open free of charge for entry into the greater Philadelphia database, $40 charge to list in the World Wide Talent Bank. Online Opportunities also handles a variety of national and Internet on-line job posting advertising services for employers.

Opportunity Network
Career Communications Group
6309 N. O'Connor Road
Suite 216/LB 26
Irving, TX 75039
214-444-0399, 800-91OPNET
modem Atlanta, GA 404-993-0050, Dallas, TX 214-444-0050

Lists open technical positions and maintains uploadable resumé database. Specialized ResumE:Mail-software available for $24.95 + $3.50 Tax & Shipping.

BULLETIN BOARD SERVICES

There are more than 50,000 bulletin boards systems (bbs) operating locally, regionally, nationally and internationally. Many contain some kind of jobs offered/wanted area as one of their features. Some bbs's operate at no charge to users (many are "hobby boards"), others offer basic services or limited access at no charge, but command fees for premium access. Many bulletin board systems which exist for niche professional groups, some operated by professional associations, also carry professional career related information. Many local bulletin boards are part of broad national/international networks that "echo" information from one to another. Amongst these homegrown networks, FidoNet and JOBNet carry significant employment related information.

BULLETIN BOARD NETWORKS

Fido Network
FidoNet has a Jobs-Now Conference devoted to all job postings, and an FJobs Conference devoted to resumés and discussions. If your local bbs carries FidoNet ask the system operator (sysop) to echo these conferences.

JOBNET

The JOBNET NETWORK, now available on over 100 systems nationwide (and growing rapidly), is devoted exclusively to jobs and employment. Andrew Walding is the driving force behind it. He can be reached through *Digital X-Connect*, Dallas, TX, modem 214-517-8443, 214-517-8315

JOBNET's conferences contain job postings, resumés and discussions organized as follows:

Job Postings:
  Accounting/Financial
  Clerical/Administrative
  Contract/Temporary
  DP/MIS (Software Related)
  Engineering/Chemical
  Engineering/Electrical
  Engineering/Environmental
  Engineering/Mechanical
  Engineering
  Health/Medical
  Human Resources
  International
  Misc.
  Professional/Managerial
  Purchasing
  Sales/Marketing
  Technical Writing
  Technical

Resumés can be posted to:
  Clerical/Administrative
  Misc.
  Professional/Managerial
  Technical/Engineering

BULLETIN BOARD SYSTEMS

Careers BBS
Miami, FL
305-828-5697

Posts local and national private sector and federal jobs. No fee required

Career Resource Center - ONLINE
2508 Fifth Avenue, Suite 147
Seattle, Washington 98121
206-233-8672
FAX 206-727-7970
modem 206-706-8217

Posts available jobs (primarily western Washington), has job-seeker/career resource bibliographies and advice files.

ECCO*BBS
modem:
    San Francisco, CA 415-331-7227
    New York, NY 212-580-4510
    Chicago, IL 312-404-8685

Free service lists national permanent and contract positions; also has resumé database.

Employment Board
San Diego, CA
619-689-1348 9600

JOBS-NOW echo and job postings for the San Diego area. No fee required.

Executive Connection
17610 Midway 134-119
Dallas, Texas 75287
modem 214-306-3393
staff@execon.metronet.com

This bulletin board service focuses exclusively on employment, careers, and business management from entry level to senior management and executive staff. It includes job listings and information on 25,000 positions—the majority are mid to upper management, scientific, engineering or MIS related—a resumé database and tons of downloadable files. There is no fee for limited access. Executive Connection also provides job posting and other recruiting services for several contingency and retainer search firms including a listserv function (listserv@execon.metronet.com) and mailing list maintenance for 7 different clients. The mailing lists include positions in sales, mis, manufacturing, medical, accounting/finance, engineering and international positions. Companies and executive recruiters can demo the service by calling via modem and logging in as first name: Company, last name: Demo, password: Guest.

FirstStep
Atlanta, GA
404-642-0665

No fee. Carries local, state, federal and Internet job listings, and has resumé database.

Georgia Online
Atlanta, GA
404-591-0777

Fee-based service carries a variety of job listings and resumé databases.

Index Systems TBBS
Atlanta, GA
404-924-4633
modem 404-924-8414, 404-924-8472, 706-613-0566
Internet: index.com

Job listings, networking and software for job-seekers. Fee for expanded access.

Infoline
Oakhurst, NJ
FAX 908-922-3937
E-mail: INFOLINE@AOL.COM
modem 908-922-4742

Local job search information and resumé database.

Jobbs
Roswell, GA
modem 404-992-8937

Lists all function positions in Southeast U.S.; also has resumé database, recruiter lists, college lists, company records.

Jobs_BBS
Portland, OR
modem 503-281-6808

Free service lists national positions in all functions.

JOBTRAC BBS
6856 Arboreal Drive
Dallas, Texas 75231
modem 214-349-0527

Free service has job listings and resumé database for all job functions, Dallas/Ft. Worth area and statewide.

Job & Opportunity Link
Chicago, IL
708-690-9860

Job listings nationwide, downloadable files. No fee required.

Opportunity BBS
Hampton Roads, VA
modem 804-588-4031

Free service primarily listing positions in the Southeastern USA; also has resumé database.

Resumé Exchange
Arctic Industries, Inc.
PO Box 9203
Scottsdale, AZ 85253
602-941-5480
FAX 602-947-4283
modem 602-947-4283

National all function, all industry vacancies listed in searchable database.

Tag On-Line Career Bank
Philadelphia, PA
modem 215-969-3845

Fee-based service posts national all function and industry jobs; also has resumé database.

ACADEMIC AND SPECIALTY

American Astronomical Society Job Register
http://blackhole.aas.org/JobRegister/aasjobs.html

Job listings for astronomers, updated monthly

Academic Physician and Scientist (APS)
voice 916-939-4242
FAX 916-939-4249
E-mail: info@acad-phy-sci.com
Internet: gopher://aps.acad-phy-sci.com

Joint effort of the Academic Physician and Scientist and the Association of American Medical Colleges (AAMC). Service lists open positions in academic medicine in the categories of: administration, basic science, and clinical science.

Academic Position Network (APN)
245 East Sixth Street
Suite 815
St. Paul, MN 55101
voice 612-225-1433
Internet: gopher://wcni.cis.umn.edu 11111

Nonprofit collaborative service lists faculty, administration, staff, graduate assistant, fellowship position announcements—primarily U.S., some Canada and Australia postings. Listing institutions pay a one-time fee, no fee for job seekers to browse APN files; files are organized by country, state or institution.

Academe This Week
Washington, DC
Internet: gopher://chronicle.merit.edu
http://chronicle.merit.edu/.ads/.links.html

Job listings from the weekly newspaper, *The Chronicle of Higher Education* are listed here the afternoon before the publication is in print. Current week listings (1,000+) are for positions with colleges and universities in the U.S., international institutions and research companies. Listings include faculty and research, administrative, executive and other positions searchable by key word or geographically.

Agricultural Job Listings
http://caticsuf.csufresno.edu:70/1/atinet/agjobs

Agricultural job postings in categories: management, sales and marketing, education, technical, research, part-time/seasonal/temporary.

American Institute of Physics
telnet://aip.org/
http://www.aip.org/aip/careers/careers.html

AIP's Employment Opportunities Database provides online access to physics and physical sciences job listings at all levels of experience. Postings, from academia, government, and industry, are updated weekly. Students can pose questions to professionals through the Physics Careers Bulletin Board.

American Mathematical Society
Internet: gopher e-math.ams.com, gopher e-math.ams.org

Professional information and opportunities for those with advanced degrees in mathematics. Positions in academe, private business and nonprofit organizations are updated frequently.

Artjob
gopher://gopher.tmn.com/11/Artswire/artjob

Postings of available jobs in the arts includes academic, artistic performance, international and internships.

Contract Employment Weekly
C.E. Publications
PO Box 97000
Kirkland, WA 98083-9700
206-823-2222
E-mail: gopher@ceweekly.wa.com
gopher gopher.ceweekly.wa.com
http://www.ceweekly.wa.com/

Searchable job listings (one set for publication subscribers, a limited subset for non-subscribers) and a lot of other information relating to contract engineering in particular, job hunting in general. 90% of jobs posted are no more than seven days old.

Delight the Customer
PO Box 303
Hudsonville, MI 48603
FAX 616-662-0192
modem 616-662-0393

Specialized job database and information oriented to marketing, customer service, sales and QA/QC. Fee required.

Direct Marketing World Job Center
http://mainsail.com/jobs.html

DM World's Job Center posts direct marketing industry job openings and resumés in searchable databases.

ERIC Clearinghouse on Assessment and Evaluation
Internet: E-mail: eric_ae@cua.edu
gopher.cua.edu

Posts jobs related to assessment, evaluation, research, statistics, and learning theory in education. The Electronic Newsletter of the Association for Institutional Research also lists its position announcements here.

International Career Employment Network (ICEN)
Indiana University, Bloomington
Internet: gopher.indiana.edu

Assistance finding jobs internationally, job listings and information for foreign nationals looking for work in U.S.

Job Openings for Economists
Vanderbilt University JOE - American Economic Association
2014 Broadway, Suite 305
Nashville, Tennessee 37203
615-322-2595
FAX 615-343-7590
gopher://vuinfo.vanderbilt.edu:70/11/employment/joe

Job postings for economists in academe, business and non-profit organizations. The American Economic Association publishes the print edition of JOE and cooperates with Vanderbilt University to produce this electronic version.

Univ. Minnesota
College of Education's
Job-Search Bulletin Board
Voice Helpline 612-626-4276
gopher://rodent.cis.umn.edu:11119/

Postings of nation-wide education positions focusing on the K-12 educational field. Includes administration, media specialty, psychology, and counseling; early childhood development and elementary education; higher education; and secondary, special, vo-tech education, and phys-ed.

COMPUTER PROFESSIONALS

Careers Online
PO Box 880
Framingham, MA 01701
voice 508-879-0700
FAX 508-875-8931
modem 508-879-4700

Free service lists computer related positions advertised in Computerworld Newspaper; also has resumé database.

Computer Careers
Charlotte, NC
704-554-1102

Specializes in DP jobs nationwide. No fee required.

Data Processing
Independent Consultant's Exchange (DICE)
D & L Online, Inc.
PO Box 7070
Des Moines, IA 50309
515-280-1144
modem:
   California 408-737-9339
   Illinois 708-782-0960
   Iowa 515-280-3423
   New Jersey 201-242-4166
   Texas 214-691-3420
Telnet to dice.com
http://dice.com

Free online job search service for engineering, data processing, technical writing professionals (9,300 active users). Companies—all brokers, headhunters and job shops—pay to put jobs on system (100–150 new jobs on and off each day). DICE averages 420 calls/day.

ISCA-BBS
Atlanta, GA
modem 404-491-1335

Information System's Consultants Association forum for the business community to contact professional consultants in the information systems field and also provides a forum for the exchange of ideas on topics of interest to information systems professionals.

J-Connection
voice 813-797-5713
modem:
   Washington DC Metro Area 703-379-0553
   South Florida 813-791-0101
   Atlanta, GA 404-662-5500

No fee to job seekers. Bulletin board service for high tech job listings, U.S. and foreign.

New Professional Network
Amherst, MA
modem 413-549-8136

Free service lists national MIS/DP, hi-tech jobs; also has resumé database.

Network World Online
modem 508-620-1178
E-mail: network@world.std.com

No fee service operated by *Network World Magazine*. Contains job listings and information and advice on career and job related issues.

INTERNATIONAL SERVICES

CyberDyne CS Ltd.
E-mail: sulocco@cyberd.demon.co.uk
http://www.demon.co.uk/cyberdyne/cyber.html

Broad listings of international job opportunities, includes links to other services.

Jobs for Africa
E-mail: webmaster@africa.com
http://www.africa.com/headhunt/

South Africa-based on-line database of CV's and open positions.

NISS,
National Information on Software and Services
gopher://gopher.niss.ac.uk:71/11/G
telnet niss.ac.uk,
select AA or AB

University job listings in the Commonwealth countries (UK, Canada, Australia, etc.)

Papyrus Media's Careers On-Line
E-mail: howard@newyork.demon.co.uk; giovanni.zanetta@ort.org
tel/fax: +44(0)171 708 4858; fax: +44 (0)171 266 4623
tel: +1 914 359 7647; fax: +1 914 359 0396
http://www.britain.eu.net/vendor/jobs/main.html

Database of International employment opportunities and information from a UK based international recruiter.

People Bank
http://www.micromedia.co.uk/ten/

Database of job seekers in the UK and Australia.
Russian and East European Institute Employment Opportunities
gopher://gopher.indiana.edu/11/theuniversity/support/reeiaie/reeiemployment

A service of Indiana University, listings in various fields for people who are seeking employment in Russia or Eastern Europe or who have expertise in the languages, history, or culture of these areas.

TeleJob
http://ezinfo.ethz.ch/ETH/TELEJOB/tjb_home_e.html

Electronic job exchange board of the Associations of Assistants and Doctoral Students of the technological institutes of Zurich (AVETH) and Lausanne (ACIDE).

TKO Personnel Inc.
2099 Gateway Place, Suite 470
San Jose, CA 95110
408-453-9000
FAX 408-453-9083
E-mail: kdr@shell.portal.com
http://www.internet-is.com/tko

Recruiting for technical (bicultural) positions, info on international careers and companies (semiconductor, software, telecommunications) in Japan, U.S. and Asia/Pacific.

ENTRY LEVEL

JobWeb
http://www.jobweb.org

Career planning and employment info, job-search articles and tips, job listings, and company information for college students, recent graduates and alumni. Also has resources for college career services and employment professionals, including career and employment information, training, and services sponsored by the National Association of Colleges and Employers, formerly the College Placement Council.

JOBTRAK
1990 Westwood Boulevard
Suite 260
Los Angeles, CA 90025
800-999-8725, 310-474-3377
FAX 310-475-7912
http://www.jobtrak.com

Over 300 college and university career centers pay to post their job opportunities, employer profiles and job hunting tips on-line for a 2–4 week period. Currently processing over 500 new job listings each day. Over 150,000 employers have utilized the service which enables them to target their job order to students and alumni at their specific choice of campuses.

University Placement Service
618-453-1047

Entry level (maybe 10% alums). Student pays $16 for resumé referral to potential employer, also has Hotline service for $25, 7 counselors in different areas. Free for employer.

MISCELLANEOUS SERVICES

Classifacts
North American Classifacts
2821 South Parker Road
Suite 305
Aurora, CO 80014
303-745-1011
FAX 303-745-1122

National database of over 40 Sunday newspaper employment classified ads. Consumer calls 800#, gets operator who searches for 3 job titles. To buy listings, pay by credit card $8.95/week (sends no more than 125 listings) + $1.85 shipping & handling. Useful service for long distance job seekers. Looking at Internet.

SBA-Online
202-205-6400 Technical Support
modem 800-697-4636
http://www.sbaonline.sba.gov
gopher://www.sbaonline.sba.gov

Small Business Administration BBS. Loaded with information for small business owners and the self-employed. No fee required.

State Employment Offices
gopher://dartcms1.dartmouth.edu:70/00/fedjobs/info/stateadr.txt

Addresses and phone numbers for all state employment offices in all 50 states.

U.S. Government Documents from the University of Missouri, St. Louis.
gopher://umslvma.umsl.edu/11/library/govdocs

Terrific collection of information for the job hunter includes: Occupational Outlook Handbooks, Small Business Administration Industry Profiles, Small Business Administration State Profiles, U.S. Census Information, U.S. Industrial Outlook, Dictionary of Occupational Titles.

4

REAL-LIFE RESUMÉS

Here they are! More than 50 resumés that have proven successful in actual job campaigns—resumés for a variety of positions, from widely diverse fields:

- Accounting & Finance
- Architecture
- Banking
- Engineering
- Entry Level
- Facilities Management
- General Management
- Health Care
- Human Resources
- Information Systems
- Insurance
- Legal
- Non-Profit
- Office Administration
- Plant Operations
- PR
- R&D/Science
- Retail Management
- Sales & Marketing
- Teaching

We've included chronological, functional, and key word resumés, and some that are a hybrid of several styles. We've made a few changes to insure confidentiality, but the resumés are otherwise unedited. What you see is what really produced results.

We've organized the resumés by primary function or industry, and added an additional "tag" to help you quickly identify those that best match your background. For example, you'll find a selection of resumés labeled *Office Administration*, with additional tags such as *Executive Support, Payroll & Benefits, Operations,* and *Data Entry*. Under *Information Systems,* you'll find resumés with labels such as *Customer Support, Design & Management, Aeronautics,* and *Database Management*.

But don't limit yourself to just resumés from your own field. Someone with a very different background may have found a way of presenting their objectives, skills, or accomplishments that will work effectively for you too. So use these sample resumés as a stimulating source of new ideas—new ways to make your own resumé stand out from all the others.

Name
Address
Phone Number

KEYWORDS: International. Willing to travel. Oil. Treasurer. Creative. Self Starter. Cash Management. Bank Relationships. Trading. Persuasive. Team leader. Credit Administration. US GAAP. Financial Reporting. Skilled Negotiator. Team Player. Total Quality Management. Forecasting. Letters of Credit. Training. Exceptional verbal and presentation skills. Results oriented. MBA finance. CPA.

BACKGROUND SUMMARY: In-depth experience in international accounting, treasury, credit, and finance. Worked and lived overseas while on permanent assignment in the Middle East and Asia. Comfortable with many diverse cultures and philosophies of doing business. TQM team leader for projects in Controller and cross-functional teams. CPA and MBA in Finance.

EXPERIENCE/ACCOMPLISHMENTS

OVERSEAS OIL CORPORATION   1972 - Present

Accounting Specialist, US GAAP	1992 - Present
Treasurer, Singapore	1989 - 1992
Coordinator Treasury, Corporate Headquarters	1987 - 1989
Financial Advisor	1980 - 1987
Coordinator, Credit Administration	1978 - 1980
Accounting Supervisor, Bahrain	1975 - 1978
Staff Accountant	1972 - 1975
Grolier Publishing International, Inc.	1971 - 1972

ACCOUNTING

- Implemented recent accounting policies for FAS 119, 115, 107, 105, and 106.

- Wrote worldwide policies, procedures and reporting requirements for Environmental Accounting.

- Created and produced an international training video for an on-line desk top publishing accounting manual resulting in reduced costs of $200,000.

- Implemented TQM improvements in the payable, delivery and ordering systems, resulting in process improvements and savings of $225,000.

- Trained local Bahrain staff in areas of general accounting, marine accounting, product costing and budgets.

TREASURY/FINANCE

- Developed and installed a PC international cash management system in Singapore which resulted in savings of $500,000.

- Established letter of credit operations in Singapore, resulting in reduced costs of $100,000 per annum.

- Negotiated full settlement of Philippine Airlines aviation receivable with unique offshore trade acceptance facility resulting in increased cash flow of $6.0 million.

- Established Islamic banking trading transactions for sales of crude oil and product into India which generated incremental profits of $750,000.

- Trained Singapore staff in cash management, credit, trade finance, and treasury operations.

CREDIT

- Developed credit policies and established credit committee for regional trading operations with sales in excess of $9.0 billion per annum, including derivative transactions.

- Supervised credit policies for 24 hour trading operations in Singapore, Japan, London, Bahrain, and Dallas.

- Managed credit policies for a Middle East refinery, resulting in maximization of crude runs for savings of $1,000,000.

- Presented credit review for Overseas Oil Corporation Directors.

EDUCATION

1985—Certified Public Accountant—Currently licensed in State of Texas
1983—MBA—Finance, Pace University, New York City, New York
1971—B.S.—Accounting, Rider College, Lawrenceville, New Jersey

PERSONAL

1990–1992 Secretary—Treasurers Club

Name
Address
Phone Number

SUMMARY

A financial manager and CPA with eight years' experience in retail and manufacturing with a Big 8 accounting firm and a Fortune 50 company. Demonstrated technical and managerial strengths include:

- General Ledger/Financial Statements
- Internal Controls
- Auditing
- Forecasting/Budgeting

- Cost Accounting
- Problem Solving
- Administration/Delegation
- Project Management

PROFESSIONAL EXPERIENCE

CONTINENTAL COMPANY - Cleveland, Ohio   **1990-Present**

<u>Manager of Accounting</u> (1992 - Present)
Manage staff of 20 to record actual results of operations, produce financial statements and maintain internal controls. Specific areas of responsibility are accounts payable, payroll, general accounting, fixed assets, and data processing.

- Transformed poor corporate audit ratings in 1991 to an excellent rating in 1993. Accomplished by planning and supervising a thorough self-audit program.

- Instituted a comprehensive account reconciliation review process which improved financial statement accuracy and enhanced accounting department reliability.

- Uncovered processing bottlenecks and reorganized workloads that resulted in producing financial statements 20% faster.

- Reduced non-exempt employee overtime 40% by providing personal computers, along with training and incentives, to develop applications.

<u>Supervisor, Planning & Analysis</u> (1990 - 1992)
Produce the annual operating plan. Prepare interim forecasts, analyze results of operations and write management reports.

- Programmed a PC forecasting model using Lotus, which compared actual profit/cost/volume performance to initial projections for a recently acquired plant. Identified key market and cost leverage points to improve profit by 25%.

- Led team of 3 analysts to provide timely variance analysis to functional managers, enabling them to resolve problems more quickly and make sound business decisions.

- Proposed mainframe system enhancement to automatically calendarize full year plan, eliminating need to manually spread and cross-foot each account.

NATIONAL ERIE CORPORATION - Cincinnati, Ohio   **1987-1990**

Financial Manager, Marketing Department (1988 - 1990)
Control and forecast $5 million Marketing Department budget. Managed staff of 3 to perform accounts payable and process vendor co-op receivables.

• Redesigned and strengthened accounting procedures, which eliminated 100% of unauthorized spending variances.

• Set-up PC information system to compare spending with sales results that promoted effective use of advertising budget.

Senior Auditor (1987 - 1988)
Perform financial and operational audits in all areas of management concern, supervise staff and communicate results of audits of both written and oral reports.

• Standardized audit procedures and workpaper formats, which increased productivity by completing six major audits (versus two the prior year).

• Supervised staff of 4 auditors to create new departmental manual.

• Identified $50,000 in advertising co-op recoveries not billed to vendors.

BEEDE & WHITE - Cincinnati, Ohio   **1986-1987**

Staff Auditor
Entry-level position auditing a variety of clients. Primary experience in health care, retail and manufacturing.

• Designed a simplified standard cost accounting method for small manufacturing client. Reduced raw material wastage by 10%.

EDUCATION

B.S. Accounting - Central Ohio University - Magna Cum Laude
Dayton, Ohio
Ohio Certified Public Accountant

PROFESSIONAL ASSOCIATIONS

Member of Ohio State Society of CPAs
Women's Society of CPAs
Beta Gamma Sigma Professional Fraternity

Name

Address   *Telephone*

CAREER SUMMARY

Over nine years of increasing responsibilities in Managerial Accounting. Proven ability in the efficient management of over 50 accounting and data entry employees, and direction of numerous projects from planning through implementation. Technical skills include, but are not limited to, profit and loss statements, budgets, forecasting and variance reporting.

WORK EXPERIENCE & ACCOMPLISHMENTS

THE PETERSON GROUP, Monterey Park, CA   **6/90-Present**

Manager of Accounting Operations   8/93-Present

Managed the operation of 50+ employees in four accounting and data entry departments, operating with a budget of $3MM, processing data for 100M commercial accounts.

- Functioned as user project leader for a computer conversion of 100M commercial accounts, resulting in improved productivity through easy access to information and improved customer service.

- Reduced the number of accounts requiring special handling by 75% through system improvements and customer negotiations, enabling a staff reduction of six employees with an annual cost savings of $150M.

- Planned and implemented use of a lockbox in the New Jersey facility, for an annual cost savings of $110M. Other benefits included faster payment application, resulting in better customer service.

- Negotiated price reduction with a lockbox vendor yielding an annual savings of $48M.

Manager of Equipment and Data Accounting   6/90-7/93

Operations management of 30 employees in two accounting and data entry departments, operating with a budget of $1.5MM, processing data for 100M commercial accounts.

- Changed lockbox vendors and operational procedures at multiple facilities, effecting an annual savings of $169M.

- Achieved an 82% improvement in production efficiencies, allowing for a staff reduction of two employees. Overtime was eliminated completely, resulting in an annual cost savings of $44M.

- Completed the conversion from manual to automated records of 15M commercial accounts, recovering $85M of revenue as well as improving customer service. The project was completed one month ahead of schedule.

BANK OF THE WEST, Los Angeles, CA   **7/89-5/90**

Financial Services Manager

Developed and analyzed budgets and forecasts with an operating budget of $4.5MM. Managed efficient and timely financial reporting to 250 clients, while servicing their 100M customers with a staff of 15 employees.

- Performed a branch audit identifying $25M of questionable administrative practices. $17M of accounts receivable over 90 days was recovered. Control procedures were implemented.

CONTINENTAL COMPANY, Los Angeles, CA   **12/80-7/89**

Manager of Accounting   10/87-7/89

Managed the Accounting Department with a staff of 20 performing general accounting duties. Financial reporting was completed through the profit and loss statements.

- Enhanced system reporting for managerial controls, enabling production, shipping and sales to better control product distribution.

- Converted to an automated inventory system providing production with greater controls, enabling quicker response to potential problems.

Office Supervisor   8/85-10/87

Accounting Clerk   12/80-8/85

EDUCATION AND TRAINING

Bachelor of Science in Business Administration
University of Southern California

Continuing Education:
USC Graduate School of Business Administration
Professional Management Program

Lotus 1-2-3, Visicalc, and Multiplan

PROFESSIONAL ASSOCIATION

Los Angeles Junior Chamber of Commerce

Name
Address
Phone Number

SUMMARY

A professional with diverse experience in the business sector for over 13 years. Major skills include strong project research capability, analysis and control, forecasting and budgeting.

ACCOMPLISHMENTS

Project Research

- Initiated and completed an inventory program, reducing audit time and improving records accuracy by 50%.

- Worked with systems programmer and organized employees to implement a payroll attendance system, resulting in cost savings of $50,000 in staff and overtime reductions.

- Streamlined monthly closing procedures and summarized documentation on computer applications.

- Assisted in the development of procedures for an awards program recognizing daily job accomplishments thus improving employee morale.

Detailed Analysis

- Completed audits and made recommendations which were implemented by the departments concerned.

- Designed spreadsheets to track labor hours and cost for department budgets.

- Analyzed historical data to determine trends and costs for annual budgets.

Forecasting

- Completed and distributed a labor and scheduling forecast on a weekly basis.

- Created an annual fringe benefit budget for 900 - 1000 salaried and hourly personnel, which was updated by quarterly forecasts.

- Maintained budgets for operating departments resulting in improved cost control.

- Created graphs utilizing computer software to track costs and determine trends for better forecasting.

-2-

EMPLOYMENT HISTORY

WESTERN BREWMASTERS COMPANY, City of Industry, CA   **1986 - 1995**
<u>Cost Analyst/Payroll Supervisor</u>   1989 - 1995
<u>Accounting/Distribution Clerk</u>   1986 - 1989

SCIENTIFIC PRODUCTS COMPANY, Irwindale, CA   **1981 - 1986**
<u>Accounts Payable Supervisor</u>   1984 - 1986
<u>Accounting Clerk/Computer Operator</u>   1981 - 1984

WESTERN SUPPLY INC., Sacramento, CA   **1979 - 1981**
<u>Accounts Payable Clerk</u>

EDUCATION

B.S. - Accounting, Union College

PROFESSIONAL DEVELOPMENT

Computer Classes in Excel, Lotus Symphony, Microsoft Word, Harvard Graphics, and Paradox

Employee Relations in Diversity Training, Team Building and Interactive Management
Personal Skills Development in Leadership and Supervisory Skills, and Communication Skills

Name
Address
Phone Number

PROFILE

Skilled Architect with expertise in leadership, concept development and project management. Excellent team member and project facilitator. Over twenty two years of experience in large scale commercial, themed and resort development, design and construction.

CONCEPT DEVELOPMENT

- Architectural planning and programming.
- Design analysis and development.
- Outline specification development.
- Presentation drawings and renderings.
- Client presentation and design buy offs.
- Design detail development.
- Master Planning

PROJECT MANAGEMENT

- Architectural programming and scope development.
- Project planning and scheduling.
- Project design and production man-hours, budgeting and estimating.
- Construction Administration
- Project scope and budget cost monitoring.
- Project staffing.
- Value engineering and cost overrun analysis.
- Building code analysis.
- Architectural Contract Documents.

EXPERIENCE

THEME PARK DEVELOPMENT INC., LOS ANGELES, CA   1988-1994

Concept Architect/ Project Architect

Responsible for a variety of development and design roles that involved project administration, management and design skills/abilities.

PROJECTS:

Fantasyland, Orlando, FL......................................Concept Architect/Lead Project Architect
Westernworld, Sacramento, CA...........................Concept Architect
Neverland, Los Angeles, CA................................Lead Project Architect
Euroworld, Paris, France......................................Project Architect/ Concept Architect
T.P.A., Tampa, FL...Concept Architect

SMITH, WATERFORD, JONES ARCHITECTS, San Pedro, CA   1986-1988

Project Manager

Managed and supervised the design development and contract documentation of a fast track project.

PROJECT:

The Watchtower, Tempe, AZ

KLEIN CUMMINGS STEWART, Anaheim, CA   1985-1986

Job Captain/Designer

Organized, supervised and assisted in design rehabilitation for the design development and contract document phase of a major Historical Register landmark hotel.

PROJECT:

> Seaside Resort, Newport Beach, CA

BARCLAY BARNES & ASSOCIATES, Westwood, CA   1983-1985

Job Captain

Coordinated, managed and supervised various phases in design and documentation stages of large scale commercial projects.

PROJECTS:

> West End Mall, Malibu, CA
> Shadowlands Mall, San Jose, CA
> Brookville Mall, San Jose, CA
> The Emporium, Albuquerque, NM
> Desert Dunes Mall, Phoenix, AZ
> Valley Mall, Reseda, CA

EDUCATION

BACHELOR OF SCIENCE IN ARCHITECTURE
Western University
Salem, Oregon

Name
Address
Phone Number

PROFESSIONAL EXPERIENCE

IMPERIAL NORTHWEST BANK, Sacramento, CA   **1988 - Present**

<u>Assistant Vice President</u>, Corporate Finance   1989 - Present

Marketed a variety of financial products to customers and prospects including interest rate hedging, asset securitization, trade finance, and private placements. Managed and provided support to a $350 million portfolio of Fortune 100 companies in a territory of nine western states. Industry specializations include Aerospace & Defense, Mining and Transportation. Built computer models for cash flow analysis and sensitivity analysis, conducted industry research, negotiated pricing and loan covenants, and performed account administration.

- Agented a $140 million structured letter of credit of a large aerospace firm. Syndicated and closed documentation within two weeks.

- Restructured balance sheet for transportation leasing firm, including refinancing of subordinated debt and new equity.

<u>Senior Associate</u>, Corporate Finance   1988 - 1989

AMERWEST BANK, Los Angeles, CA   **1986 - 1988**

<u>Corporate Banking Officer</u>, Commercial Real Estate

Managed a construction real estate portfolio of $4 million. Backup account officer for a real estate portfolio of $450 million, assisting in credit analysis, analyzing construction expenses, and leasing cash flow analysis.

- Set up database program for researching and tracking the development of prospective customers.

- Completed the Commercial Banker Development Program.

EDUCATION

UNIVERSITY OF SOUTHERN CALIFORNIA, Los Angeles, CA   1986
Bachelor of Science, Business Administration (Emphasis in Finance)

COMPUTER SKILLS

Proficient in Lotus 1-2-3, WordPerfect, Windows.

Name
Address
Phone Number

SUMMARY

Executive with broad, in-depth experience in engineering management and business development. Key accomplishments in the following areas:

- Development and growth of successful engineering organizations
- Marketing of new business, resulting in major sales to key clients
- Regional office management with full P&L responsibility

Recognized as:

- A leader with the ability to motivate people and stimulate creativity
- Innovative problem solver with demonstrated success at setting and achieving goals
- Having an entrepreneurial spirit with acute business development skills
- Being adept at organizing, directing and implementing programs, managing multiple projects and establishing strong client relationships

PROFESSIONAL EXPERIENCE

CBA CORPORATION   **1985 - 1994**
Engineering services firm with over $160M annual sales to utilities and industrial clients.

Vice President   1990 - 1994
Member of executive management team and total quality/cycle time improvement steering committees, resulting in a 20% improvement in gross profit margin over a 2-year period. Held electrical/I&C Chief Engineer position (staff of 185) responsible for $24M annual sales, development of strategic business plans and market assessments, and marketing of new technologies. As Regional Manager, had complete P&L responsibility for 300-staff office with annual revenues of $30M.

- Sold a competitively bid $40M power plant design scope; achieved 98.8% of performance incentive fees over 2-1/2 year period.
- Reduced regional office overhead costs by 30% over 12-month period.
- Achieved a key $3M award of new integrated software engineering application for a major West Coast utility.
- Sold a $1M project to analyze instrumentation loops for optimizing setpoints and calibration intervals.

Division Manager   1988 - 1989
Led three separate divisions: Operations, Systems Engineering and Business Development.

- Developed a Midwest utility into a major client through initial $1M sale of power analysis work.
- Sold a $3M scope for the mechanical, electrical and structural design of a new pulp-and-paper facility.
- Directed aggressive marketing efforts resulting in a 50% increase in sales over 6 months.
- Achieved 25% improvement in revenue over 9-month period while turning around an unprofitable division.

<u>Section Manager</u>   1985 - 1988

Responsible for marketing, technical quality, recruiting, training and technology development for a new electrical/I&C engineering section.

- Built an engineering staff from 3 to 60 in 3 years, producing over $5M in annual sales.
- Sold a power plant control room upgrade scope to a Midwest utility, generating over $8M in revenue.
- Developed power analysis as a new business area, resulting in over $12M in sales to 15 clients.
- Contracted first Regional design projects at five key Midwest clients.

HI-TECH ENGINEERS   **1982 - 1985**

Engineering services firm with over $40M annual sales to utilities.

<u>Engineering Manager</u>

Developed an electrical/I&C staff of 25, marketing and engineering plant modification design projects up to $1M in value throughout the Midwest and Central U.S. Also functioned as the national business development manager for fire protection and hydrogen injection systems and as project manager for several multidiscipline projects.

HAMILTON ENGINEERS   **1975 - 1982**

One of the largest U.S. engineering services and consulting firms with over $200M annual sales to utilities.

As an Electrical Engineer, promoted to Project Engineer in 1980, responsible for design, equipment specification, client and vendor interface, and environmental qualification review of several plant systems for new facilities as well as major backfit modifications.

MOTOR CORP. USA   **1973 - 1974**

Second largest U.S. automobile manufacturer with facilities worldwide.

Electrical systems and component design engineer; member of Management Training Program.

EDUCATION

Master of Engineering, University of Kansas, 1973
B.S. Electrical Engineering, University of Kansas, 1973

PROFESSIONAL AFFILIATIONS

Institute of Electrical and Electronics Engineers
Instrument Society of America
American Nuclear Society

REGISTRATIONS

Registered Professional Engineer in
Illinois, Indiana, Iowa, Kansas, Louisiana
Michigan, Minnesota and Wisconsin

Name

Address   *Telephone*

OBJECTIVE

Senior level position in key staff, internal consulting, strategic planning or acquisition team leading to possible new business and/or P&L responsibilities. The position will utilize Chemical Engineering, Manufacturing and Industrial education and experience. Overseas assignment or relocation to Europe is acceptable.

SUMMARY

Professional engineer with over 18 years of broad experience in the chemical manufacturing industry. Assignments have included start up, managing and acquiring new technology and plants in both European and United States locations.

MAJOR ACCOMPLISHMENTS

New Business and Technology Transfer

- Accomplished target companies analysis for an acquisition strategy including financial, marketing, technology and human resources evaluations, resulting in a $17 million acquisition.

- Developed new business relations and organized an engineering department with cash flow forecast, financial reporting and project scheduling, through a $5 million capital investment, resulting in a technology transfer between Europe and the U.S. after a business acquisition.

- Designed and implemented a $10 million, three-year capital investment for a newly acquired company, developing concurrently a manufacturing analysis based on computer simulation and a team-based decision procedure. This resulted in a P&L improvement of $2 million/year and a reduction in capital requirements of $5 million.

Management

- Designed and planned a corporate culture change based on Dr. E. Demming's philosophy, statistical process control implementation, and participative management approach for a corporation of 360+ employees and $70 million revenues. This produced a sales increase of $4.4 million and profit improvement of $840 thousand.

- Turned around a 6000 TPY, $15 million revenue of a bi-oriented polypropylene film plant; the two-year program improved P&L by $3 million, reduced staff by 40%, increased production by more than 60%, and established customer confidence in product quality.

Engineering/Technical

* Installed the first waste copper-ammonia recovery plant; this is now a $40 million/year business and the leader in Europe.

* Developed and implemented critical path plan for ammonia reformer replacement. This $4 million project was accomplished ahead of schedule and under budget.

PROFESSIONAL HISTORY

CHEMCO, Brussels, Belgium   **1981-Present**

    Metals Inc., Baltimore, MD   1993-Present
    Vice President, Operations and Engineering
    Special Project Manager

    Metallurgical Chemicals Corp., Galveston, TX
    Engineering Manager   1992-1993

    Filmco, Liege, Belgium   1990-1992
    Plant Manager

    Metals Inc., Baltimore, MD   1986-1990
    Engineering Manager

    Sortoma, Tertre, Belgium   1981-1986
    Project Engineer
    Field Supervisor, Engineering Department
    Production & Products Development Engineer

INSTITUT FRANCAIS DU PETROLE, Rueil Malmaison, France   **1980-1981**
Multi-client market study and fellowship.

EDUCATION

Universite de Souerain, Belgium (1980)
    Civil Engineering Degree in Chemistry

Institut Francais du Petrole, France; Fellowship (1981)

PERSONAL

Fluent in French

Name
Address
Phone Number

Professional Objective

An entry level position in international banking

Education

State University of New York at Buffalo, 1994. Concentration in international relations/political science. 3.4 GPA (4 point scale). Additional courses in computer sciences, French and Spanish.

State University of New York at Purchase, summer 1994. Graduate level courses in marketing, corporate finance, intermediate accounting and federal taxation.

Honors

Graduated Cum Laude from State University of New York at Buffalo.
Dean's List six out of eight semesters.
Phi Eta Sigma, Freshman Honor Society
Pi Sigma Alpha, National Political Science Honor Society

Experience

Research Assistant, Psychology Department, State University of New York at Buffalo. Assisted in coding and analyzing data from various studies. Results pending publication. Winter 1993-1994.

Bank Teller, New York Savings, Cornell, N.Y. Managed and processed financial transactions. Gained knowledge of banking procedures. Summer 1993.

Manager (part-time), La Maison, a woman's clothing store, Broadalloin, N.Y. Supervised employees, managed daily financial transactions and developed public relations skills. Summers, school holidays, 1991-1993.

Computer Skills

WordPerfect, Microsoft Word, Lotus 123, Aldus Pagemaker,
Claris Filemaker Pro

Co-Curricular Activities

Writer, The Spectrum. Researched and wrote feature articles, covered sports activities for student newspaper.

Name
Address
Phone Number

OBJECTIVE: A position in hotel management with opportunities for advancement.

EXPERIENCE:

Summer 1993   **Hotel Kenilworth, Pittsburgh, PA**
Banquet Captain
Managed large functions including business meetings, weddings, and other social functions. Responsibilities included identifying customer needs and delivering quality customer service through the coordination of service and kitchen personnel activities.

Summer 1992   **Creative Food, Pittsburgh, PA**
Caterer
Organized function space at various meeting locations according to client specifications. Responsibilities included designing food station displays and serving/supervising designated areas.

Summer 1991   **Casino Royale, Las Vegas, NV**
Room Service Captain
Supervised room service personnel to ensure courteous service to hotel guests and promote a positive working environment. Additional responsibilities included preparing weekly payroll and schedules, as well as catering special events on the Hotel and Casino yacht.

EDUCATION: **University of Ohio, Columbus, OH**
Bachelor of Science May 1994
Major: Hotel, Restaurant, and Travel Administration

Activities: Hotel Sales Marketing Association Club
UOhio representative for N.Y. Hotel Show
Intramural Softball 1992-1994

COMPUTER SKILLS: WordPerfect, Lotus 123, and dBase III

Name
Address
Phone Number

OBJECTIVE

To obtain a part time or full time Human Resource position to apply my skills that have developed through my Merrill Education in the HR field.

EDUCATION

Merrill College, Thompson, VT
Major: Business Management

RELEVANT COURSES

Interpersonal Relations in Management
Human Resource Management
Personnel Policy (Class devoted to training development and evaluation)

EXPERIENCE

Bank Teller, Summers, June 1992 - Jan. 1995
North Bank, Brattleboro, VT
Handled personal/commercial banking activities in a "local" banking atmosphere. Worked primarily as a line teller; also assisted in the personal Loan Servicing and Accounting departments. Responsible for clerical, data entry, and administrative assistant duties in these departments.

ABILITIES

Extensive computer/PC experience via the Merrill College computer network. Applications/software used includes:
WordPerfect for Windows
Lotus 1-2-3
E-Mail Account

ACTIVITIES

Disk Jockey-WMRL Merrill College Radio: Sept. 1990-Present.

WBTY Executive Board Member: Calendar year 1992, 1994
Position Held: Music Director

Name
Address
Phone Number

Keywords

- Budgeting
- Cost Control
- Energy Management
- Facilities Management

- Fire/Safety Systems
- Housekeeping
- Office Services
- Operations

- Preventative Maintenance
- Project Management
- Property Lease Management
- Purchasing

- Security
- Staff Supervision
- Team Player/Builder
- Vendor/Contractor Management

Career Objective

Facilities Manager and/or Operations Manager for a mid to large-size business organization where experience-based competence is needed.

Summary of Qualifications

Demonstrated leadership, initiative, and the ability to plan, organize, and manage facilities operations activities. Achieved a reputation to complete projects with on-time proficiency and cost savings. A responsive and accomplished professional who enjoys a variety of challenging projects and responsibilities. An effective manager with skills in budgeting, project management, and team building. High energy level, conscientious, dependable, and a strong work ethic.

Professional Experience

THE REGISTER, SANTA ROSA, California   1987-1995

Facilities Manager
Managed facilities department, serving a 2,600 employee organization. Responsible for budgeting, security, purchasing, preventative maintenance, housekeeping, project management, space planning, vendor/contractor performance evaluation, contract administration, and staff growth and supervision.

- Built a highly motivated and proactive facilities administration team of 2 to 7, in two years streamlining departmental guidelines and procedures, converting manual systems to computerized automation systems, producing significant improvements in the performance and efficiency of the department, including contractors and vendors.

- Developed a facilities division annual operating budget of $10.6 million. By creating the budget, $325,000 in waste was identified and eliminated over a two-year period.

- Planned, negotiated, selected and managed contractor to retrofit all lighting systems for a 435,000 square foot production plant and a five-story office building, resulting in a projected annual energy savings of $354,000 a year and a nine month return on investment.

- Negotiated and selected new security and janitorial companies, resulting in a combined savings of $253,000 a year, and at the same time upgraded the quality of service.

- Planned, developed and executed the consolidation of 70 leased offices/warehouses under the management of the facilities division, reducing rental and maintenance expenses, improved budgeting process, and ultimately combined and reduced rental properties to 26 facilities.

- Conceived and implemented a centralized purchasing program, reducing purchasing expenditures by $135,000 a year, while eliminating employee pilferage.

- Under severe time constraints and the possibility of losing critical data, was successful in assembling and managing a team of engineers, contractors, and in-house personnel to complete a flawless data center power distribution upgrade on schedule and within budget.

- Established program to test, monitor, and verify that monthly, quarterly, and annual fire suppression systems are operating effectively, meeting all local, state, federal and insurance regulations.

THE HITCHING POST, Fort Collins, Colorado   1983-1987

Newsprint Manager
Managed all newsprint operations; purchasing, ordering, inventory control, warehouse management, newsprint and insert hauling contract negotiations, waste, budgets, company and corporate reporting, and managed a union paper handling department. In addition, managed all rental properties, hazardous waste, and the coordination and reporting of Operations Division budget performance.

- Successfully set up a computerized budget performance report, tracking, forecasting and reporting a $315 million annual operations division budget, providing weekly and monthly reports to top management.

- Reduced newsprint handling and transit waste 15% by implementing strict roll handling procedures with contracted hauler and suppliers, resulting in improved press runs and a savings of more than $200,000 a year.

- Successfully served as an appointed member of a $58 million production plant task force, advising and assisting on newsprint warehouse facility, material handling equipment, waste systems, equipment and operational procedures.

- Studied, developed, and implemented a hazardous waste program, placing the company in full compliance with all EPA regulations, while reducing the company's liabilities.

- Eliminated labor intensive waste disposal methods and procedures, saving $75,000 a year in landfill and waste hauling charges.

- Successfully negotiated waste service agreement, generating $50,000 a year in added revenue.

- Saved $95,000 a year by identifying and eliminating excessive paper warehousing.

THE MORNING NEWS, Houston, Texas   1963-1983

Newsprint Supervisor   1980-1983
Supervised newsprint department: ordering, inventory control, quality control, transportation/traffic, reporting costs, and supervision of personnel.

Plant and Purchasing Assistant   1974-1980
Responsible for purchasing supplies and materials, office equipment, office furniture, and newsprint. Supervised plant department: security, purchasing, housekeeping, stockroom, PBX, and cafeteria. Managed postal mailroom operations, including the hiring and training of personnel.

Buyer/Newsprint Clerk   1969-1974
Responsible for purchasing activities and maintaining newsprint records and reports, and accountable for newsprint quality program.

Newsprint Records Clerk   1963-1968
Responsible for maintaining accurate newsprint records and reports.

EDUCATION

Attended Arlington State College
Arlington, Texas

PROFESSIONAL AFFILIATIONS

International Facility Management Association, IFMA
Building Owners and Managers Association, BOMA
Association of Professional Energy Managers, APEM
Newspaper Purchasing Management Association, NPMA

Name
Address
Telephone

CAREER SUMMARY

Human Resources/Employee Relations Manager with over 17 years of experience in all areas of people management and development in manufacturing and service industries.

EXPERIENCE AND ACCOMPLISHMENTS

MORSE ALLOYS COMPANY, Atlanta, Georgia   **1985-1994**

Employee Relations Manager   1987-1994

Responsible for managing the Employee Relations function for five to seven plant work sites in the aluminum extrusion, casting and finishing industries.

- Developed and implemented "Quality of Work Life Program," which resulted in a 15% reduction in supervisory work force while maintaining production standards.

- Introduced "Quality Circle Program" at casting facility which realized more than $800K in savings the first year of the program.

- Directed successful company campaigns against union organization attempts in 1988 and 1991.

- Established a maintenance department testing and certification program that resulted in reduced turnover and a 10% improvement in equipment downtime.

- Directed an in-house security investigation that uncovered and eliminated over $40K annually in illegal vendor practices.

- Successfully resolved 100% of EEOC cases without litigation or settlement cost to company over 7-year period.

- Developed and conducted management training programs for front-line supervisory personnel, which resulted in a substantial decrease in employee/supervisory confrontations and improved employee morale.

Employee Relations Representative   1985-1987

Responsible for delivery of labor, training, employment, benefits, safety and security programs for the manufacturing plant and five regional sales offices.

- Processed union grievances through arbitration. Successfully presented arbitration cases with 100% resolution with company's position upheld during 2-year period.

- Established a Safety Program for the manufacturing plant, reducing lost-time cases by more than 50% during the first year.

- Successfully negotiated resolution of several OSHA citations and fines, reducing company's exposure by more than $200K.

- Headed Corporate Safety and Health Review Team at the Louisville (KY) packaging plant. Review was responsible for significantly reducing company's exposure to regulatory agency fines and employee safety and health risks.

SOUTHEAST TRANSIT, INC., Atlanta, Georgia   **1983-1985**

<u>**Manager of Employment**</u>

Responsible for all employment and personnel policy administration for 2,100 employees. Maintained personnel record center, internal promotion procedures, medical program, relocation program, and wage and salary administration.

- Established national recruiting program that resulted in the placement of 36 engineers, architects, etc., in positions that had been open for up to 2 years.

PARCEL SERVICES, INC., Atlanta, Georgia   **1973-1983**

<u>**Employment Manager**</u>

Responsible for all employment services for 2,500 employees in 38 locations within the state of Georgia. Also responsible for medical programs, employee orientation/training programs, employee problem resolution/communication programs, affirmative action and compliance and workplace union contract interpretation.

<u>EDUCATION AND PROFESSIONAL DEVELOPMENT</u>

B.A., Psychology, MOREHOUSE COLLEGE   **1976**

- Completed degree requirements at night while working full-time.

Numerous professional training courses and workshops in all areas of human resources management.

Name
Address
Phone Number

SUMMARY

Over thirteen years of broad based human resources and contract administration experience at Fortune 500 Headquarters and Division Operations. Especially skilled in Administrative Services, Employee Programs Management and Employee Relations. Outstanding communication skills, high levels of resourcefulness and creativity, and a powerful level of initiative and energy. Extremely effective negotiator and able to motivate and persuade while working in a team environment.

PROFESSIONAL ACCOMPLISHMENTS

Employee Services and Programs

- Instituted a "Lunch and Learn" parenting skills' series offering a "no cost" educational opportunity to employees and their families.

- Established and implemented an Employee Assistance Program, assisting employees with emotional or financial issues, exhibiting company's proactive stance towards employees' personal needs, and providing a healthier and productive workforce.

- Coordinated 20 major and 160 regular group outings, for employees and families to meetings, cultural and sporting events for groups numbering up to 6,500 individuals.

- Created company-wide ethnic holiday, tradition, and festival programs responding to the needs of and creating an understanding between a multi-cultural workforce.

- Developed and implemented a National Eldercare Research Library and skills enhancement program, eliminating unnecessary "emergency" out of town trips, reducing "at work" research phone time by 80%, and increasing productivity of employees needing help or support with eldercare issues.

Creative Planning

- Developed a Staff Community Involvement Program (SCIP), increasing voluntary participation by employees in community projects and providing positive company visibility in the community and requests for company involvement in selected charities.

- Supervised design and layout of two full service cafeterias, coordinated and chaired focus groups, and created marketing package for grand opening.

- Designed and developed a fully staffed and equipped fitness center, including a full-scale aerobics program, creative promoting, first year enrollment exceeded membership goal by 85%. Monthly subsidy was reduced by 95%.

- Managed the design and development of an on-site child care center for 159 children, insuring ADA and state licensing compliance.

-2-

- Researched, developed, and implemented the EASY PAY debit card system for use in the cafeterias, vending machines, and company store. Utilization rate of 37% exceeded original objectives by 19%, reducing extended employee lunch hours from an average of 1.5 hours to 45 minutes.

- Devised and implemented a company-wide flyer distribution system, eliminating one head count and saving 85,000 pieces of paper per month.

- Through creative marketing and upgrading cafeteria and catering menus to include a wide selection of healthier food choices, increased sales by $120,000 annually and reduced company subsidy to 15.9% from 35.6% the previous year.

Negotiation

- Located and converted unusable space to accommodate a planned company store. Successfully negotiated a 75% reduction in the initial bid.

- Designed RFP, coordinated bid process, and negotiated contract for temporary help, reducing costs by $35,000 annually.

- Qualified and negotiated fee arrangements with search firms, resulting in annual savings of $110,00.

- Negotiated monthly management fee for company fitness center, reducing expense by 18%.

WORK EXPERIENCE

GENERAL SERVICES INC., Ventura, CA   **1990 - Present**
Staff Services Manager, Human Resources
Managed staff of 113 in-house and contract employees. Formulated and managed $3.8 million budget. Responsible for the design, development, implementation, and overall management of corporate support services.

TEMPSERVE, Ventura, CA   **1985 - 1990**
Branch Manager
Managed operations of two branches with 5 direct reports and 300 contract employees.

DRAKE CORPORATION, Thousand Oaks, CA   **1983 - 1985**
Personnel Recruiter
Recruited employees, evaluated skills, provided new-hire orientation and completed termination process for entire division.

COMPUTER TECH SERVICES, Thousand Oaks, CA   **1980 - 1983**
Personnel Representatives
Specialized in EEO and employee relations.

FRIENDS ACROSS AMERICA, Camarillo, CA   **1975 - 1980**
Public Relations Specialist
Managed event planning and corporate relations.

EDUCATION

Abraham Lincoln, San Veda - Diploma

PROFESSIONAL DEVELOPMENT

Founding Member and President, Gold Coast Chapter of NESRA
Leadership/Effective Communication, Sterling Institute, 1992
Working with Difficult People, Amgen, 1991
Business Finance for Non-Financial Managers, AMA, 1993

CERTIFICATIONS

CESRA (Certified Employee Services and Recreation Administrator)
Certified Counselor - EAP
Charter Member of Conejo Valley Employers Child Care Task Force
Public Speaking Engagements on Family Friendly Cultures

COMPUTER SKILLS

MacIntosh, Wordperfect 5.1, Word 5.1, Excel

Name
Address
Phone Number

KEYWORDS PROFILE

Culture Change • Change Management • Organizational Alignment • Process Reengineering • Turnaround Operations • Performance Management • Downsizing • Personal Coaching • Facilitation • Team Building • Leadership • TQM • 360 Degree Feedback • Succession Planning • Upward Appraisal

OBJECTIVE

OD consultant opportunity that utilizes my skills and experiences in operations management, training and development, organization development, personal coaching, process facilitation, and culture change management.

SUMMARY

Over 25 years of outstanding achievement in key operations and staff positions within, as well as consulting externally to, Fortune 500 companies: managed start-up and turnaround divisions, developed and delivered executive and management development programs, and designed and implemented organizational culture change initiatives.

PROFESSIONAL HIGHLIGHTS

Organizational Development

- Facilitated an in-depth organizational evaluation providing a detailed plan for initiating culture changes within a major health care company. Conducted intensive, week-long seminars for over 300 Vice Presidents, Directors and Managers who received 360 degree feedback on their management practices and developed individual goals that were incorporated into their next performance appraisal.

- Conducted initial Vice President meetings to model and instill practices of good communication and collaboration across the various business divisions and corporate departments. These meetings doubled as assessments allowing for leadership skills to be exhibited and for identifying those who were on board with the new culture.

- Wrote an Executive Succession Plan adopted by the CEO and senior executives that provided for regular assessment of management talent and depth as well as plans for retaining and developing key performers, correcting weaknesses in management depth and future growth needs.

- Developed a process for communicating organizational changes likely to disrupt employees that achieved more rapid assimilation and acceptance with minimal downtime or lack of productivity.

Management

- Reengineered health insurance operations division creating core process teams replacing functional departments: customer results turned around from unacceptable performance to results greater than national industry standards within ninety days.

- Managed a complete turnaround in a key market of company-run stores for a $12 billion plus retailer re-staffing and training a management team that increased sales and gross profit margins, improved store image and service, and reduced controllable expenses, taking the lowest rated market from ninth to first ranking within two years.

- Upgraded the management programs and trainer skills at a Fortune 50 Corporate Training and Development Center, increasing the target populations, tripling the staff, and setting new standards for trainee achievement, trainer productivity, and positive client feedback.

- Reduced division infrastructure and support costs by $7 million while improving service results and individual productivity.

Training and Development

- Trained quality teams to work on key areas of noted weakness within a managed care division, achieved national accreditation.

- Conducted customized management training to support a culture shift from hands-on control methods to facilitation and coaching methods, allowing managers and supervisors to empower their employees.

- Completed formal training needs assessment for a critical functional area that was underperforming. Cross-trained employees in areas of skill and knowledge deficiency through key performer coaching as well as the development of on-line training materials and job aids, resulting in improved cycle times, fewer errors and reduced employee turnover.

- Centralized national training function, reducing staff by 31% and costs by $6 million while improving the quality of program delivery.

- Developed and implemented a training center system for managing the delivery of technical and management courses for 30K+ employees. Integrated the design, development, delivery and evaluation of training.

PROFESSIONAL EXPERIENCE

CONSULTANTS GROUP, Houston, Texas   1990 - Present

Senior Partner

Management training and consulting services: implement culture change initiatives, including assess organizational climate, develop model aligning mission, vision, goals and values, restructure size and scope of functional responsibilities, re-engineer work units to achieve core process ownership, identify key management practices, conduct feedback-driven seminars, and coach "on-line" inside divisions to help managers and employees shift their day-to-day focus and behavior.

SOUTHWEST CORPORATION, Houston, Texas   1978 - 1992

Staff and Operations Management

Fourteen years of progressive promotions and ever-widening responsibilities, including Operations and Staff positions both in the field and at the Corporate Headquarters. Managed field operations in franchise - California and Nevada - as well as in corporate-owned - Virginia and Florida - areas. Broadened line experience with staff time in Merchandising - Sales Manager and Buyer - and Human Resource departments - Corporate Training Center Manager and OD Consultant.

REGIONAL NORTH HIGH SCHOOL, Mission Viejo, California   1967 - 1977

Teacher, Counselor, Administrator

English and Social Studies teacher involved in all facets of English curriculum, including TV, film making, photography and journalism. Taught and created materials for over thirty classes across all four grade levels from the learning disadvantaged to Advance College Placement students. Chaired workshops on writing instructional objectives. Produced school yearbook and faculty newsletter. Coached baseball and basketball teams.

EDUCATION

B.A.:   San Jose State - English/Social Studies

Post Degree: California Secondary Teaching Credential

Post Graduate: Over 75 units in Administration, Counseling, Education, English, and Psychology

Professional: Certifications to conduct numerous training programs from such companies as Forum Corporation, Learning International, Karass, Inc., American Consulting and Training, University Associates, Vanguard Group, Zenger-Miller, Wilson Learning, and others.

Instructional Systems Design credential from San Diego State.

PROFESSIONAL

Member, Board of Directors, International Board of Standards for Training, Performance and Instruction
IBSTPI

Member, National Society for Performance and Instruction   NSPI

Member, American Society of Training and Development   ASTD

Member, Society for Human Resource Management   SHRM

Name
Address
Phone Number

SUMMARY

Eighteen years experience in all areas of the employee benefits field at a major financial institution with 40,000 employees. Demonstrated skills in benefit plan design, regulatory compliance, mergers, acquisitions and divestitures, plan administration for both welfare and pension benefits, and staff management.

ACCOMPLISHMENTS

BANK SECURITIES INCORPORATED   **1974 - 1993**

Vice President, Human Resources Department

Health and Welfare Benefits

- Designed a benefit system to implement and administer a broad-based cafeteria style flexible program. Produced all communication materials for implementation for 35,000 employees.

- Produced communications package to introduce health care program for 25,000 employees.

- Designed system to implement and provide on-going administration of a flexible benefits program for 6,000 retirees including production of individualized enrollment materials.

- Designed and implemented a mainframe record keeping system for COBRA that streamlined the function and reduced staff.

- Automated interfaces for benefits data for 40 different subsidiaries of the corporation.

- Implemented new employee benefits accounting procedures and database system that streamlined the function and reduced staff.

Pension Benefits

- Reconverted a profit sharing plan to a thrift savings plan and systems design, enrollment and communications.

- Designed and implemented changes to a defined benefit pension plan to comply with TEFRA, DEFRA, ERTA, and REA.

- Converted a thrift savings plan to a 401(k) plan including plan design, systems, communications, and enrollment.

-2-

Acquisitions, Merger, and Divestitures

- Implemented flexible benefits program and pension program at 20 acquired companies including all plan analysis, plan design, communications (both print and video), training, systems modifications, and enrollment.

- Designed benefit system conversion, shut-down, and archival of database of over 100,000 employee and retiree records to facilitate company merger.

Regulatory Compliance

- Updated employee benefit plan documents for all plan changes and annually produced required Summary Plan Descriptions and Summary Annual Reports.

- Produced required IRS filing annually.

CAREER PROGRESSION

Vice President, Benefits Planning   **1990 - 1993**

Vice President, Flexible Benefits   **1987 - 1990**

Vice President, Benefits & Compensation   **1985 - 1987**

Vice President, Pension & Thrift Unit   **1981 - 1985**

A variety of positions, all within the benefits division, of
increasing responsibility leading to the Vice President position.   **1974 - 1981**

Name
Address
Telephone

OBJECTIVE

Profit and loss responsibility as a member of the senior operating management team of a medium-sized firm or a division of a large corporation.

SUMMARY

During an 18-year career with Hilland Companies, established a solid record of performance in series of increasingly responsible line management and senior staff positions -- $10 million to $80 million in sales. Among strengths are analytical, communication and decision-making skills in both domestic and international business environments.

PROFESSIONAL EXPERIENCE

HILLAND COMPANIES, INC.   **1976-Present**

Hilland Latin America, **Miami, Florida**   **1989-1994**

Regional Vice President with profit and loss responsibility for a group of diverse international subsidiaries. Business activities in the following areas: dairy, ice cream, confectionery, bakery and snacks. Sales Revenue: $80 million/year. Employees: 4,000.

- Acquired assets of a bankrupt snack food company. Negotiated favorable terms with creditors, installed new management and developed entirely new marketing strategy; as a result, the company was profitable within 6 months. (Business is currently earning in excess of $900,000/year.)

- Sold two unprofitable subsidiaries, providing a net U.S. tax benefit to the parent company and eliminating $1 million in consolidated operating losses.

- Directed the conversion of a chain of 250 independently owned, licensed retail outlets into a complete franchise system. The modernized image, marketing programs and quality control systems were self-financing and helped increase the number of outlets to 400 in 3 years, reversing a weakening market share trend.

*   Achieved a $100,000 annual savings through the reduction of regional office expenses.

Hilland International Food Division, Chicago, Illinois   1985-1989

Division Controller responsible for financial reporting and analysis of a $1 billion division.

*   Directed the design and implementation of an automated management information reporting system utilizing satellite communications between division and overseas offices. System substantially improved compliance with month-end reporting requirements.

*   Instituted a series of regional controllers' conferences, achieving improved communication and cooperation between various levels of a world-wide financial organization. An improvement in the quality of monthly and year-end reporting resulted.

*   Developed ·a systematic monthly reporting format that greatly improved the accessibility of financial data to the division president and other key managers.

Hilland Corporate Office, Chicago, Illinois   1976-1985

*   Developed a simplified standard cost system that was installed in six company branches.

*   Designed and implemented an automated system for processing company-wide fixed and leased asset records. The system was in use for 15 years, accommodating a four-fold increase in the size of the corporation.

*   Wrote the first corporate policy manual, bringing together all the policies issued over many years; thus providing a format for the future release of additions and changes.

EDUCATION

B.S., Management and Administration, Indiana University, School of Business, Bloomington, Indiana.

Name
Address
Phone Number

SUMMARY

Executive with extensive strategic planning and leadership experience with Fortune 500 manufacturing companies, in the domestic and international arena.

Principal strengths include:

- Solid background in logistics, procurement, material and production control.
- Excellent communication skills.
- Ability to coordinate complex operations.
- Fluent in Spanish, Portuguese, Italian, conversant in French.
- Broad knowledge of international cultural backgrounds.
- Proficient in computer software tools.

CAREER HIGHLIGHTS

- Participated in the strategic planning which led to the implementation of semi-conductor manufacturing facilities in Curacao and Portugal, with 2200 employees and annual production of $100 million.

- Acted as internal consultant to a calculator company's Italian facility. Improved shipping, line item performance, cycle time, and working inventory. Deliveries increased 250% in five years.

- Reduced inventory $10 million by devising and implementing reports and establishing policies to analyze raw material and finished goods' inventories.

- Managed the operation phase-out of two large business ventures in the field of home computers and time products, minimizing material liabilities and optimizing inventory utilization.

- Led the planning, logistics and customer services support for a newly established calculator division in Portugal.

- Conceptualized and authored planning, import/export and production control procedures for a company's overseas manufacturing which are still in use after 21 years.

- Composed and edited Spanish and Portuguese manuals and speech products for Latin American markets.

- Reorganized and restructured scheduling and production control of automobile factories and managed 50 operatives to procure and provide efficient and cost effective material flow, with an output of 300 units/day.

- Directed and implemented a full integration of planning systems and procedures between two automobile manufacturers, after a corporate merger.

EMPLOYMENT HISTORY

ACI INCORPORATED   **U.S.A.**   **1968 - 1994**
- International Planning and Procurement Manager
- International Material Coordinator
- Production and Material Planning Supervisor
- Production and Material Control Manager   **Portugal**
- Operational Manager
- Import Planning Coordinator   **Germany**
- Inventory and Production Control Supervisor **Curacao**
- Purchasing and Import/Export Supervisor

INTERNATIONAL PACKAGING   **Argentina**   **1967 - 1968**
- Programming and Methods Manager

AMCAR   **Argentina**   **1964 - 1967**
- Production Planning and Specification Manager

INTERNATIONAL MOTOR COMPANY   **Argentina**   **1959 - 1963**
- Schedule and Material Control Supervisor

EDUCATION

B.S. Business, Madrid University, Spain

PROFESSIONAL DEVELOPMENT COURSES

- Six Sigma Manufacturability
- Process Reengineering
- Customer Focus
- Production and Inventory Control
- Management
- Team Effectiveness
- Quality Control
- Electrical Circuits

****
U.S. Citizen

Name
Address
Phone Number

SUMMARY

Contracts Manager with extensive experience in complex business transactions, contracts, negotiations, software/hardware licensing agreements, procurement and project management. A unique blend of legal and business experience with an outstanding record of sound business judgment, expanding responsibility and achievement across multiple functions. An excellent teacher and communicator. Builds a solid, highly motivated team.

EMPLOYMENT HISTORY

SCIENCE INSTRUMENTS COMPANY   **1990 - PRESENT**
Manager, Contracts

Provide business support, contract management and procurement of supplies and services for the Information Engineering Facility with $500M in annual sales. Principal negotiator with the authority to bind the corporation. Supervise contract administration, program planning and financial management for multi-year contracts. Develop and review proposal data for major programs. Resolve contractual and audit disputes.

- Negotiated numerous complex corporate Software Licensing Agreements with Fortune 100 Companies.

- Developed business practices and contracts for the Federal Sales Group which grew in annual sales of software and services from $500K to $35M.

- Ensured the legal protection of intellectual property and proprietary data.

- Negotiated a $350M Proposal with EDS to support the Department of Defense.

- Captured several targeted programs with an initial combined value of $125M by executing Strategic Alliance Agreements and Teaming Agreements.

- Received "Top Performer" Award 1993.

- Negotiated a Joint Development and Marketing Agreement with ABC Corporation.

- Negotiated a Software Distribution Agreement with INC.

GENERAL DEFENSE COMPANY   **1988 - 1990**
Financial Manager

Responsible for contract administration, financial management and pricing functions for five large contracts. Managed operating trends by preparing and analyzing financial reports involving revenue, expense and schedule variations.

Supervisor, Contract Administration   **1986 - 1988**

Supervised contract administration function, proposals and change orders for a large government contract.

SPACE TECHNOLOGY, INC.   **1984 - 1986**
Attorney, NASA Contracts

Responsible for contract compliance, change orders and modifications for a large NASA contract with an Award Fee and Incentive Fee structure.

US ARMED FORCES   **1976 - 1981**
Captain, Combat Control Team

Leader of a Combat Team that conducted special operations for the Military Airlift Command.

EDUCATION

Juris Doctorate, 1984 - California Western School of Law
Master of Arts, 1978 - Webster University
Bachelor of Arts, 1975 - Baylor University

ASSOCIATIONS

American Bar Association
Federal Bar Association
Utah State Bar Association
National Contract Managers Association

Name

Address   *Telephone*

SUMMARY

Over 20 years of experience in long-term health care management and operations, from administrator of a skilled nursing facility to senior division manager of a major nursing home corporation.

PROFESSIONAL EXPERIENCE AND REPRESENTATIVE ACCOMPLISHMENTS

HEALTH CARE CORPORATION, Portland, Oregon   **1983-Present**
Owns, operates, and manages intermediate care facilities and retirement housing complexes in 39 states with gross revenues in excess of $1 billion annually.

Senior Vice President of Operations   1992-Present
Directed the management, development, and operations of the Western Division, consisting of 120 facilities with 2 regions, 13,000 beds, and annual operating budget of $260 million.

- Co-ordinated start-up of 16 new nursing facility projects with 2,000+ beds and total project costs in excess of $80 million.

- Restructured and streamlined regional operations, reducing overhead costs by $400,000 annually.

- Launched development of company-wide rehabilitation department improving operating results and enhancing marketing posture while increasing quality of rehabilitation programs at facility level.

- Reduced accounts receivable over 60 days from 16.0% to 8.0% in first year by implementing intensive training programs and offering incentive programs.

- Led a successful hands-on effort to turn around a 60-facility region that had experienced extensive bottom-line losses, federal and state survey problems, and high staff turnover.

- Supervised start-up, marketing program, and operations of the first specifically designed facility for the care and treatment of victims of Alzheimers Disease -- a $10 million, 148-bed facility.

- Implemented updated salary structure program for middle management and regional staff that led the company to review/ update salary administration programs company-wide.

Vice President of Operations - Mt. States Region   1991-1992
Managed 56 facilities in 8 northwest states. Responsible for development of 3 year business plan and operating budget of $120 million annually. Directed 2 regional vice presidents and 20 support staff on quality assurance programs, marketing, capital budget review, and development of specialty programs.

- Developed and trained new operation managers in company systems in a region that experienced acquisition growth of 40% (22 facilities) in 18 months, strengthening their ability to reduce operating losses and increase regional profits.
- Introduced a new specialty service wing in a facility that solved a 2-year occupancy problem, as average census went from 75% to 96% annualized.

Regional Vice President - So. California/Arizona   1986-1991

Responsible for daily operations of 32 facilities. Planned operating budgets, quality assurance compliance, employee relations programs, and recruitment. Supervised 3 District Directors and regional staff.

- Reduced administrator turnover from 60% to zero over 2-year period -- best record in company.
- Established administrator orientation program that served as model for company.
- Increased net operating profit an average of 20% annually over 3 years.

District Director   1984-1986

Managed 8 western facilities.

Area Administrator   1983-1984

Managed 1 facility, supervised 3.

PREVIOUS EMPLOYMENT

Administrator of 80-bed skilled nursing facility.   1977-1980

Administrator of family-owned skilled nursing facility.   1973-1977

MILITARY

U.S. Army - Medical and Dental Corps   1963-1972

EDUCATION

Masters of Business Administration - Health Care Management   1984
City College, Portland, Oregon

Bachelor of Arts - Business Administration   1983
City College, Portland, Oregon

PROFESSIONAL AFFILIATIONS

Licensed Nursing Home Administrator
American College of Health Care Administrators

Name
Address
Phone Number

SUMMARY

Seasoned technologist with over 15 years experience as a lead analyst in the Data Processing/Information Services profession. Major strengths are in managing, designing and implementing enterprise systems. Additional skills in leadership, budgeting, planning and project management. An innovative leader with excellent communications and interpersonal skills who gets results.

Languages:
C, C++, Visual BASIC, 80X86 Assembly, FORTRAN
Operating Systems:
DOS, Windows, VMS, HP-UX, RTE-A
Data Base Management Systems:
Paradox, Access, dBase, Oracle, Ingres
Hardware Systems:
IBM-PC, VAX, HP-9000, Tandem VLX, HP-1000

PROFESSIONAL EXPERIENCE

EXPRESS SYSTEMS COMPANY, Houston, Texas   **1994 - 1995**
Market leader in retail payment systems (money order sales)

Director of Technical Services

Budgetary responsibility for 3 cost centers - $1.8 MM. 4 managerial direct reports. 24 x 7 data center operations, 5 computer operators, systems manager, technical specialist, software development staff (3 Tandem programmers, 2 DataCard terminal programmers). Warehouse and inventory management operations involving over 40,000 POS terminal systems.

- Facilitated the team that moved a legacy application from a network model DBMS to a relational model. Decreased by 75% the programming time necessary to respond to special reporting requests.
- Directed the effort of a team in the development of data center operations policies and procedures reducing off-hours support calls by 50%.
- Led the effort to out-source a logistics and repair operation that resulted in a reduction of shipping errors by 80%, and decrease of repair time by 30% with no increase in cost.
- Negotiated and managed the in-sourcing of a programming effort that saved the company over $100,000 per year.
- Designed and implemented a peer teaching program that gives each development programmer the opportunity to present to his or her peers those things which he or she does best. This encouraged team work, and enriched the job of each participant, leading to 0% turnover and redundant expertise within the existing organization.
- Instituted the use of automated software development management tools to better track the progress of and measure the true cost of development projects, for the first time this gave an accurate assessment of project status.

ANALYTICAL SYSTEMS CORPORATION, Colorado Springs, Colorado   **1992- 1994**

Manager of Information Services

Time spent 50-50 on management and development. Responsible for analysis automation applications, data center operations, network and telecommunication administration, equipment repair and user help desk. Staff of 5 direct reports.

- Utilized Borland C/C++, The Resource Workshop and Windows to design and develop several applications that automated analyses that were previously done manually. These applications were networked via PathWorks and accomplished automatic data base update and report generation.
- Established Visual BASIC as the standard development tool for GUI development to adapt turn-key systems from instrument manufacturers to the specific needs of the laboratory.
- Conceived and instituted a customer survey and feedback system where the internal customers of programming staff products had a voice in setting the priority and direction of the IS department as a whole.
- Instituted the use of automated software development management tools to better track development projects.
- Rewarded for job performance by receiving several "one-time" incentive awards (i.e. - paid weekend retreat).

COLCO, Arvada, Colorado   **1991 - 1992**
Check Guarantee and other Financial Services

System Manager

Systems technical specialist for HP-1000 (11 CPUs) and HP-9000 (2 CPUs) data center. LAN Administrator and internal coordinator for all telecommunication service providers (Nation wide 1-800 user help desk, and X.25 transaction network).

SOLID STATE ELECTRONICS, Aurora, Colorado   **1985 - 1991**
Market leader in pressure sensor, radiation-hard memory, and ASIC semiconductors.

Principal Software Engineer

Designed, coded, tested and maintained production testing system used for interim and final test of solid-state pressure sensor product line, much of which is still in use today.

MILITARY SERVICE

Four years active duty - United States Army - Fort Bliss, Texas
Discharge with rank of Captain

EDUCATION

MBA Information Systems - University of Colorado, Colorado Springs, Colorado
(GPA 3.58) - Earned degree from AACSB - accredited curriculum while working full time.
BS Chemistry - Ohio Tech University, Akron, Ohio

PROFESSIONAL TRAINING

Completed certification in the use of Scitor's PS/6 (project management software system)

Name
Address
Phone Number

SUMMARY

10 years extensive professional and practical experience in problem analysis and solutions, supervising workflow, managing, designing applications, documentation development, team playing, customer relations, training and motivation.

EXPERIENCE

TECCO, Sacramento, California   **1989 - 1994**
International Sales Administrator, Technical Support Representative

- Through an (800) support line answered a heavy volume of questions regarding the technical aspects of Tecco software eliminating customer's downtime.

- Analyzed customer problems and worked independently and with a team to come up with viable solutions and recommendations.

- Assisted customers with the installation of Tecco mainframe and Professional Tecco software; in fine tuning software, setting-up drawing file management and interfacing software with third-party plotters.

- Processed orders and acted as a liaison between international Tecco subsidiaries, their resellers and corporate headquarters worldwide resulting in increased goodwill and timeliness.

XYZ, INC., Sacramento, California   **1984 - 1989**
Product Support Engineer, Senior Support Representative, Marketing Support Representative

- Supported all aspects of XYZ equipment and software through account management calls while interfacing with administrators which assisted in better corporate communication.

- Conducted numerous communications tests, instructed customers in use of asynchronous/synchronous communications software resulting in less down time.

- Tested and maintained communications hardware and software between P.C.s and mainframes utilizing UNIX systems and electronic publishers.

- Worked closely with field engineers in troubleshooting hardware and software problems which improved operational communications.

EDUCATION

Master of Arts, Business Education, California State University, Los Angeles, California.
Bachelor of Arts, California State University, Los Angeles, California.

PROFESSIONAL DEVELOPMENT

Networking, Introduction to Programming (UCLA), 2D/3D Design Installation (basic and advanced classes) Data Management - CADAM.
UNIX System Administration, OASIS System Administration, Electronic Publishing - NBI
Introduction to VM/CMS Basics - IBM

TECHNICAL SKILLS

Languages:
    EXEC, TURBO PASCAL

Operating Systems:
    Window 3.1, AIX, BSD, VM/CMS 6.0, MS-DOS

Environments:
    Networking Topologies - Ethernet, SNA, Novell, Token Ring, Gateways, Bridges; IBM mainframe including familiarity with large systems, utilities, operating system usage, editors; UNIX workstations.

Installations:
    Engineered - 2D/3D Design; NBI OASYS Product Line - Office Automation, Communications, Electronic Publishing. Software on PC's and on UNIX Systems; Microsoft Windows (PC), Ethernet -cabling, TCP/IP software (PC's). System and PC Configurations: customer application development.

Hardware:
    IBM and compatible Personal Computers, IBM 5085, 5088, Risc, Sun Sparc, Versatec color and black/white plotters, Calcomp electrostatic plotter, HP pen plotter, Gerber photoplotter, HP LaserJet Printers, Postscript printers, Hayes and compatible modems, scanners.

Software:
    Microsoft Word for Windows, Microsoft Excel for Windows, WordPerfect, Lotus 1-2-3, Legende, CADAM V3R2M0 and V2R1M1 2D/3D Design, Data Management, Accounting, Statistics Hardcopy, ISD, NC2, Access, GIM, CADEX/CADPC, CPR's; V3R1M0 ProCadam Software: ISPC 2.1; Versatec Random 1.1 and VHC; Multiplan, Team-Up Energraphics.

Name
Address
Phone Number

SUMMARY

Thirteen years experience in resolving customer real time software and hardware problems via the phone and on site support through assessment of situation and by expediting resolution resulting in customer satisfaction. Broad expertise in operating systems and communication software. Special talent in setting up large office automation projects, including personal computers and mini-computers. Excellent customer communication skills.

EXPERIENCE

COMPUTER SERVICES, Los Angeles, CA   1981 – Present

Software Support Engineer   1987 – Present

Perform phone and on site support for hardware engineers and customers. Responsible for complete software support:

- Operating systems - RDOS, AOS, AOS/VS, UNIX, XENIX, MSDOS

- Computer languages - Business Basic, Assembler, Pascal, C

- Data Base Management Software - SQL, INFOS, DG-DBM

- Communication software and systems - LAN/WAN, XODIAC, XTS, SNA, BLAST, TermManager and PCI, TCP/IP, NFS

- Office automation systems - CEO (Comprehensive Electronic Office), PC integration office

- Implemented installation and testing of new software releases for major customers. Conducted large network installation based on 3COM TermServeres and TermManagers software in the integration with IBM PC's and DG super mini-computers.

- Established various facets of system security features such as: ACL (Access Control List) charts, CLASP utility and system MONITOR software.

- Performed on-site software troubleshooting for large customers.

Field Support Specialist   1983 – 1987

- Participated in planning and selecting of the hardware and software to be used in office automation projects as a computer system support specialist.

- Provided support for planning of on-line real time computer systems, to record and analyze large masses of information simultaneously using Personal Computers with mini-computer hosts which acted as a file server.

- Coordinated and managed two hosts on a multinational network in conjunction with a variety of vendors.

-2-

Computer Field Engineer   1981 - 1983

- Installed and maintained proper operation of processors and wide range of disk subsystems, tape drives and printers.

L.E.M., Moscow, Russia   1977 - 1981

Computer Engineer

- Designed complete systems based on Minsk-68 (Motorola 6800 eq.) Microprocessor to control and trace analog signals.

- Simplified a system to expedite handling of computer data. Complete hardware and software design.

EDUCATION

B.S. Electronic Engineering/Computer Design, University of Moscow, Moscow, Russia

Data General Certificates:

- Eclipse & Nova Systems
- MV Eclipse & RT Eclipse Computers
- RT Operating System Programming
- AOS/AOSVS System Manager/Support
- SNA/X.25 System Manager
- Comprehensive Electronic Office
- PC Integration System Programming

Name
Address
Phone Number

PROFESSIONAL SUMMARY

A hands on electronics test engineer with a practical common sense approach to troubleshooting and system/subsystem testing. Always a team player in tune with company and project goals. Over seventeen years combined experience in numerous engineering and test disciplines. Especially skilled in the following areas:

➡ RF Systems/Subsystems Testing.　　➡ Test Procedure development.

➡ Automated Electronic Testing.　　➡ Electronic Design, Fabrication and Test.

➡ Analog & Digital Circuitry.　　➡ Stabilized Sight Systems.

➡ Test Requirements Planning.　　➡ Laser and Thermal Imaging Devices.

➡ Data Collection and Analysis.　　➡ Servo Mechanisms.

• Security Clearance - Secret (D.I.S.C.O.)

PROFESSIONAL EXPERIENCE

1981 - PRESENT

Astronautics Incorporated, Los Angeles, CA
Positions Held: Lead, Test Planning Analysis (TPA) Requirements and Procedure Development; Engineer, Senior, Logistics; Engineer, Senior, Test Operations.

✔ Led the Installation and Checkout Activity (I&CO) effort for complex RF Support Equipment and Facilities RF System Hardware tests. All equipment was installed, tested and certified ahead of schedule and under budget. Received commendation and cash award for strict adherence to test disciplines and professional excellence.

✔ Researched, developed and produced the first test procedures used on the Peacekeeper Flight Test Program. The procedures became the company standard for further procedure development.

✔ Performed as Launch and Test Team member. All areas of responsibility were performed flawlessly, resulting in 100% mission success.

✔ Established and maintained the check and balance system for test requirement compliance for all procedures utilized for Receipt through Launch Processing. Process instilled customer confidence and satisfaction. Received Quality Award of Excellence.

Page 1 of 2

1975 - 1981

Aircraft Incorporated, Los Angeles, CA - Electro-Optical and Data Division
Positions Held: Test Engineer 1; Associate Engineer; Electronic Technician 'A'.

- ✔ Selected as Engineering Field Representative to England (British Aerospace Company, Filton, England). Performed the Installation and Checkout of Automated Test Stations and provided classroom training to British engineers and technicians. Received employee commendation and promotion.

- ✔ Redesigned two manual Electro-Optical Test Positions into one automated Test Position resulting in substantial cost savings, efficiency and production increase.

- ✔ Repaired and prevented the scrapping of an Automated Circuit Card Test Station by innovative repair methods. Normal operation was restored and saved the company over $250,000.00 in replacement costs. Was selected 'Technician Of The Year' and was promoted to the engineering staff.

- ✔ Reduced Test Position 'Down Time' by 70% by implementing Electrostatic Discharge precautions during maintenance activities and sinking chemical grounds at susceptible locations. Production output increased by 15% (received commendation).

PRIOR EXPERIENCE

Power & Light, Detroit, Michigan - Journeyman Lineman 'A'. Active
in the installation/maintenance of overhead and underground primary/secondary power lines.

EDUCATION

Smith Institute of Technology, Akron, Ohio - Graduated, diploma received
(Electronics Technician).

Jefferson College, Las Vera, CA.

Work related classes in Computer Sciences and Business Administration.

COMMUNITY SERVICES

Treasurer of Homeowner Association.

Former fund raising chairman - Operation Big Brother.

Prior Department Representative for company U.S. Savings Bond and Blood Drives.

MILITARY SERVICE

United States Marine Corps - Honorably Discharged. Viet Nam Service Veteran.

Page 2 of 2

Name
Address
Telephone

SUMMARY

Broad management experience in Information Systems. Exposure to a broad range of technology. Excellent management, marketing and technical experience complemented by an M.B.A.

BUSINESS EXPERIENCE

NICHOLSON CORPORATION - St. Louis, Missouri   **1993-Present**
An international manufacturing company.

Vice President Information Systems
Responsible for Information Systems/Telecommunications planning, research, consulting, operations, development, support, budget of $10 million and supervision of 80 professionals. Key management programs and business systems included:

- Developed Strategic Information Systems Plan, which recommended a distributed processing technical architecture and resulted in reducing Information System costs (IBM 3081, IBM AS400, IBM PS/2, SNA, TOKEN RING, T1)

- Recommended implementation of a Computer-Integrated Manufacturing System, reducing production cost and inventory (IBM AS400, IBM PS/2, MAPICS/DB)

- Initiated a project to implement a Computer-Aided Selling System, reducing selling cost and increasing sales effectiveness (IBM 3081, COMPAQ LAPTOP, DBASE IV)

NATIONAL BRANDS, INC. - St. Louis, Missouri   **1980-1993**
An international consumer products manufacturing company.

Director Information Systems   1991-1993
Responsible for Information Systems planning, research, consulting, operations, development, support, budget of $20 million and supervision of 120 professionals. Key management programs and business systems included:

- Directed implementation of a Computer-Integrated Manufacturing System, reducing production costs and shortening order lead time (IBM 3084, AS400, IBM S38, IBM PC, IMS DB, ASI, STSC, PRISM, ON-SPEC, COBOL)

- Directed the selection and implementation of a Marketing Decision Support System that dramatically improved the efficiency of advertising and promotions (IBM 4381, IBM PC, TOKEN RING, Express, Easytrac)

- Increased staff productivity by 10% with implementation of a system development methodology

- Formed quality assurance group, which provided guidelines and measurements that increased quality by 10%

Manager New System Development   1985-1991
Responsible for new systems, major enhancements to existing systems, budget of $4.0 million and supervision of 40 professionals. Key management programs and business systems were:

- Directed the implementation of an Advertising and Promotion Accounting System, which supported cost control (IBM 3084, IMS DB, COBOL)

- Directed the implementation of a distributed processing Total Maintenance System at 13 plants, reducing inventory costs by $1.0 million and increasing production uptime (IBM 8100, DMS, COBOL)

- Directed the implementation of a Retail Distribution Information System, which increased productivity and resulted in more effective advertising and a 20% improvement in out-of-stock conditions (IBM 3084, Telxon 701, COBOL, TECAL)

- Directed the implementation of a Financial Planning System that resulted in more effective pricing decisions (IBM 3084, IBM PC<, IFPS)

- Directed the implementation of Office Automation Systems that increased productivity 20% (IBM 3084, IBM S36, DEC Vax, Wang VS, IBM PC, SNA, DW4, Lotus)

Supervisor, Systems and Programming   1982-1985
Lead Analyst/Programmer   1980-1982

SHARED COMMUNICATIONS - Cincinnati, Ohio   **1975-1980**
Computer service bureau. Functioned as account sales manager.

DONLIN CORPORATION - St. Louis, Missouri   **1974-1975**
An international aircraft manufacturer. Functioned as a systems analyst/programmer.

EDUCATION AND PROFESSIONAL TRAINING

M.B.A., Finance, Xavier University   1980
B.A., Math/Physics, Western Illinois University   1974

Effective Executive Program - Wharton Business School   1993

Speaker: Data Processing Management Association: 1989
                Estimating Systems Development
            RAMIS User Conference: 1982
                Marketing Information Systems

Author: "Marketing Information Systems," *Computer World*   1983

Name
Address
Phone Number

SUMMARY

A seasoned professional with extensive experience in information technology. Major strengths in evaluating, selecting, and negotiating appropriate database management systems. Additional skills in streamlining and analyzing software management and quality control.

PROFESSIONAL EXPERIENCE

FAB INCORPORATED - Houston, Texas   **1982 - Present**

Account/Technical Manager   1990 - Present

Responsible for the delivery of proposals including software review and pricing, substitute proposals, the assessment of the technical fit, how to configure the systems, vendor negotiations, and the conversion to/from software. During the conversion responsible for any technical issues that arise, schedules, and serve as the focal point of communications for the client.

- Managed the consolidation for four out-sourcing clients to a centered date center that resulted in $2 million increase in annual revenue.
- Developed and implemented a process for software functional review that eliminated redundancy and produced annual savings of $100K.

Manager, Database Systems   1984 - 1990

Managed and directed the efforts and activities of nine systems programmers who maintained IMS DB/DC, CICS VS, TOTAL, and DB2 and Oracle on VAX. Responsibility for company-wide reliability, availability, and service for the above sub-systems including response time, goal setting and delivery of that service level. Responsibilities also include related vendor package justification, installation, and support of products such as ADF II, OMEGAMON, AOF, BTS, and INTERTEST. Budgeting responsibility, performance review, AFE preparation, and all other administrative duties required to manage a department.

- Implemented standards and practices for product quality that resulted in an annual reduction of service goal failures by 25%.
- Directed a research and development project for Database Management Systems which provided more timely and accurate information that expedited standardization across multiple computing platforms.

Manager Software Quality Assurance   1982 - 1984

Managed a department of three database analysts to insure on-line performance standards adherence. Developed and maintained a design review methodology, performed purchase package reviews, reviewed all database technology AFE's, performed database design consulting, performance and tuning of databases, managed performance standards committee.

INDEPENDENT CONSULTANT - Dayton, Ohio   **1979 - 1982**

Performed logical and physical design of IMS DB customer databases for a public utility company. Developed and trained programming staff for coding of IMS DB programs.

SMITH DEPARTMENT STORES - Dayton, Ohio   **1978 - 1979**

Senior Database Analyst
Performed logical and physical design of IMS financial databases. Responsible for all support of these designs.

ELECTRO CORPORATION - Corning, New York   **1974 - 1978**

Project Leader
Responsible for the design, programming and installation of an IMS DB system for customer order and billing. Responsibilities included logical and physical design, installation and support of all developed software including IMS code.

MEDCO - Green Bay, Wisconsin   **1972 - 1974**

Senior Programmer/Analyst
Responsible for design, coding, installation and maintenance of the Customer Billing System. Additionally designed and implemented the Budget Reporting System.

UNIVERSITY OF MINNESOTA - St. Paul, Minnesota   **1969 - 1972**

Programmer
Responsibilities included support of the Budget and Payroll Systems in addition to the design and implementation of a Food Stuffs Bidding System for the University food service.

EDUCATION

University of Iowa, Iowa City, Iowa
B.B.A. January 1969

Name
Address
Telephone

SUMMARY

Over 20 years of insurance industry experience, adept in market and organizational analysis, planning, and providing leadership and training. Experience includes personal lines underwriting and agency marketing for personal, commercial, and financial service products for a multi-state territory of independent agents.

CAREER HISTORY

MUTUAL INSURANCE COMPANY   **1974-Present**

A $12.5 billion multi-line national company providing insurance protection to individuals and businesses.

AGENCY OPERATIONS MANAGER - Minneapolis, MN   1992-Present

Managed company liaison with 35 independent agencies responsible for production and retention of $8 million in personal/commercial lines and financial services business. Improved agency relations by working with and training agency principals.

* Designed and implemented business plans and analyzed agency operations to obtain increased company production and improved loss ratios. Overall production increased by 10% and profitability by 6% within one year.

* Established cross-selling programs for personal lines through the use of telemarketing and computer-assisted software programs, which improved production 15% each year.

* Introduced and trained agency staff in the use of company software and personal computer, significantly increasing operational efficiency and agency production.

* Established program to realign unprofitable agents, improving state-wide loss ratio by 20%.

* Developed new sources of production, resulting in the appointment of three new agents and increased production of over $1.3 million in Casualty-Property premiums.

AGENCY MANAGER - PERSONAL LINES, Minneapolis, MN   1992-1994

Developed/managed $10 million of personal lines business with over 125 agents in Minnesota, North Dakota, and Wisconsin. Budgeted/monitored expenses, analyzed product and profit results, and developed action plans for regional manager. Improved company/producer relations and achieved mutual profit and production goals.

- Developed and implemented territorial marketing plans and strategy, resulting in growth of over 50% within two years.

- Planned and directed a personal lines sales campaign at a summer resort attended by 20 agents. Sales increased by 25% over the previous year.

ASSISTANT AGENCY MANAGER, Minneapolis, MN   1985-1990

Managed and developed 45 agents in Minnesota and Wisconsin with over $3 million personal lines. Motivated them by direct personal contact, use of incentives and sales aids, recommended selection, appointment and promotion.

- Initiated and managed training program for agents, improving selling techniques, underwriting, product knowledge, and understanding of company procedures.

- Analyzed marketing territory demographics and made strategy recommendations for pricing and market penetration. This resulted in the appointment of 18 new agencies and an increase of 37% in personal lines business.

ASSISTANT MANAGER - PERSONAL LINES, Omaha, NE   1979-1985

SENIOR ACCOUNT ANALYST - PERSONAL LINES, Omaha, NE   1977-1979

ACCOUNT ANALYST - PERSONAL LINES, Des Moines, IA   1974-1977

ENVIRO, INCORPORATED, Minneapolis, MN/Des Moines, IA   **1973-1974**
$1.5 billion manufacturer of consumer and institutional cleaning products.

DISTRICT SALES MANAGER

SALES REPRESENTATIVE

EDUCATION

B.S., Business Administration, Minnesota State University   1972

Series 7 (NASD)   1993

Certified Insurance Counselor (CIC)   1995

Name
Address
Phone Number

KEY WORD SUMMARY

Risk Management. Planning. Negotiating. Property Policies. Casualty Policies. Deductible Plans. Retro Plans. Cashflow. Loss Forecasting. Budgeting. Subrogation. Surety Bonds. Certificates. Contracts. Loss Experience.

SUMMARY

Assistant Risk Manager/Department Supervisor with in-depth knowledge and experience in the evaluation, analysis, and the various methods of handling corporate risk exposures. Special expertise in negotiating pricing and terms of property and casualty policies and associated responsibilities connected therewith. Heavy experience with deductible and "retro" plans and other cash flow programs. Also skilled in loss forecasting and the preparation and administration of insurance budgets and premium allocations.

PROFESSIONAL EXPERIENCE

CONVENIENCE INCORPORATED   1970 - 1995
Nation's largest Convenience Store Operator and Franchisor with annual sales in excess of $6 billion.

Assistant Risk Manager

Working independently with a staff of seven and in close conjunction with the Corporate Risk Manager, was responsible for performing the various managerial and planning duties and the decision-making responsibilities associated with the "Risk Management" function of the corporation.

- Negotiated with workers' compensation carrier and was successful in convincing them to write their first multi-state deductible program which resulted in reductions of premium taxes and assigned risk charges in excess of one million dollars.

- Developed and managed the preparation of the corporation's annual multi-million dollar property and casualty insurance budget and made expense allocations to the company's various operating divisions based on loss experience and exposure.

- Evaluated and analyzed the corporation's insurance reserves (in excess of 100 million dollars) to ensure adequacy when compared to outstanding insurance liabilities and was responsible for the explanation and presentation of same to upper management and the corporation's external auditing firm.

- Negotiated and reached final agreement with excess liability carrier regarding amounts due in excess of Aggregate Stop Limit. Efforts resulted in a net return of $740,000.

- Managed the process in arriving at the amicable resolution and settlement of several multi-million dollar property and business interruption losses.

- Managed the payment and proper amortization of all insurance premiums and invoices.

- Initiated and implemented subrogation efforts against third parties causing property damage to the corporation. Efforts resulted in an average of $50,000 to $100,000 of recovery per year.

<u>Assistant Risk Manager</u> (continued)

- Implemented a new bonding program to cover lottery obligations in the State of Virginia. Program resulted in continuing annual savings of approximately $40,000.

- Instituted process to consolidate various surety bonds thereby reducing cost of bond premiums by 20%.

- Negotiated contracts with service companies regarding the providing of claims service on workers compensation and liability claims.

- Developed and implemented procedure to be followed by staff in paying pro-rata insurance premiums to lessors of the corporation which generated annual savings of approximately $100,000.

- Foresaw the need for new programming to assist in the streamlining of the issuance of insurance certificates. Arranged for the programming to be completed, tested, and implemented thereby saving countless hours of clerical expense.

- Developed procedure to be followed by field management and corporate staff when franchisees exercised their option to obtain separate insurance programs.

- Developed procedure to be used in calculating Franchise Indemnification Credit which was a contractual obligation of the corporation to provide to its independent franchisees.

- Set up format/plan to be used in reconciling and tracking of insurance accruals by corporate division and policy year.

- Conducted and presented training seminars on insurance issues in lease and sub-lease contracts covering real property.

EDUCATION

Richland College, 1980
Southern Methodist University, 1976
University of Arkansas, 1969

OTHER TRAINING/AFFILIATIONS

Insurance Manager Program in Long Grove, Illinois.

Insurance Institute of America Certificate Program in general insurance.

Associate Member - Dallas Chapter of RIMS

Name
Address
Phone Number

SUMMARY

Five years as senior in-house counsel at a Fortune 100 company with substantial experience in public and private financings and securities law. Over four years of corporate practice with a major New York law firm. Demonstrated ability to analyze business transactions for legal risks and recommend solutions. Innovative and cost effective in approach to issues.

PROFESSIONAL EXPERIENCE

HILLAND CORPORATION, Houston, Texas   **1986 - 1991**

<u>Counsel</u>   1988 - 1991
<u>Senior Attorney</u>   1986 - 1988
Advised corporate finance and banking departments concerning joint ventures, leveraged leases, divestitures, loan agreements, letters of credit, Chapter 11 and general corporate matters. Directed in-house attorneys and support staff for designated projects. Supervised in-house tax and leasing attorney.

- Represented company in completing complex $170 million leveraged lease financing for steel subsidiary's joint venture with Japanese partner. Advised Treasury department regarding compliance with covenants of lease and security documents.

- Organized "Debt Room" containing a copy each of the company's 65 public and private debt instruments, related prospectuses and bound volumes. Analyzed each instrument to determine whether debt was senior, subordinated, secured, unsecured or guaranteed. Analysis formed basis for classifying debt in company's plan of reorganization and for negotiating settlement of debt claims.

- Resolved over 350 secured and unsecured claims totalling more than $5 billion, including public senior and subordinated debt, in the company's Chapter 11 proceedings.

- Researched applicable facts and law and managed outside counsel to obtain temporary restraining order and permanent injunction after Iraq's 1990 invasion of Kuwait to prevent fraudulent draws on over $7 million of letters of credit issued on behalf of a subsidiary to an agency of the Government of Kuwait.

- Participated in preparation of Forms 10-K and 10-Q and compliance with SEC reporting requirements.

- Directed outside counsel for various corporate finance, workout, bankruptcy and general corporate matters.

- Drafted or reviewed general corporate contracts, including contracts for cash management, software licensing, telephones and office space.

ROGERS, STEWART, MCCARTHY, New York, New York   **1981 - 1985**

<u>Associate</u>
Broad range of experience in corporate law including public offerings, private placements, partnership agreements, leveraged leases, mergers and acquisitions and securities regulation.

- Met client deadlines to document business transactions; advised clients of legal risks and suggested solutions; maintained high Cravath standards of practice.

<u>Associate</u> (continued)

- Closed over $__ million of public offerings and $__ million of private place-ments, including preparation of required SEC filings, official statements or offering memoranda.

- Selected as senior associate to prepare documents required for merger of two "Big Eight" accounting firms.

- Performed key role in foreign parent company's acquisition by tender offer and short-form merger of outstanding minority interest, valued at over $6 billion, in major U.S. oil company.

FIRST BANK, New York, New York	1976 - 1979
<u>Loan Workout Department</u>	Summer 1979
<u>Metropolitan Term Loan Department</u>	1977 - 1978
<u>Factoring and Finance Division</u>	1975 - 1976
CITYBANK, Raleigh, North Carolina	1975 - 1976

<u>Credit Analyst</u>

EDUCATION/PROFESSIONAL DEVELOPMENT

J. D. (1981), Raleigh Law School, Raleigh, North Carolina

- Comment Editor (1980-81) and Associate Editor (1979-1980), *Raleigh Law Review.*

Master of Business Administration (1975); Bachelor of Art, Mathematics (1973); University of North Carolina, Chapel Hill, North Carolina.

- Phi Beta Kappa; Beta Gamma Sigma; North Carolina Business Foundation Scholar (Top 10% MBA Class)

<u>Attended the following seminars:</u>

Banking and Commercial Lending Law (ALI-ABA) 1990; Dealing with the S.O.B. Litigator (ABA Satellite) 1989; Developments and Trends in Environmental Law (Sidley & Austin) 1988; Twenty-first Annual Uniform Commercial Code Institute (UCI) 1988; Letters of Credit: A Workshop for Bankers (World Trade Institute) 1988.

PROFESSIONAL AFFILIATIONS

Member, State Bar of Texas and New York State Bar; Admitted to practice before the Supreme Court of the United States; American, Texas and Dallas Bar Associations.

Name
Address
Phone Number

PROFESSIONAL EXPERIENCE

CONVENIENCE STORES INCORPORATED   **August 1983 - 1992**
Houston, Texas

The world's largest convenience retailer and, until the late 1980's, the largest independent gasoline distributor in the United States, the largest fragmentary ice manufacturer in the world, one of the largest dairy product distributors in the United States, the operator of nationwide food production and distribution centers and one of the nation's largest auto parts retailers, with annual sales of $12 billion and approximately 60,000 employees.

<u>Attorney in the office of the General Counsel</u>: Acted as lead counsel in a broad range of international license agreements, real estate transactions, trademark matters, state regulatory and environmental issues and general contract matters. Coordinated outside counsel in major litigation concerning real estate, bankruptcy and contract issues.

• Negotiated license agreements and designed financing arrangements for the construction and operation of convenience stores in Norway, Hong Kong, Australia, Ireland and the United Kingdom.

• Acted as lead counsel on the divestitures and acquisitions of corporate properties.

• Negotiated and drafted manufacturing and distribution agreements, license agreements and private label agreements

• Coordinated all trademark applications, renewals, licensing and related litigation for the company's 1200 trademarks including foreign and domestic products and services.

• Coordinated the applications, renewals and related litigation for the company's alcoholic beverage, tobacco, lottery and food stamp licenses through the company's leveraged buy-out, two corporate felony convictions, bankruptcy and reorganization. Succeeded in retaining all licenses.

• Negotiated all contractual matters related to pay telephones for approximately 3,000 stores and major office equipment for numerous division and field offices.

• Served as counsel to The Employees' Trust in matters concerning IRS compliance.

• Presented the company's alcoholic beverage compliance programs to the National Conference of State Liquor Administrators at national and regional meetings.

• Council Member, International Law Section, State Bar of Texas.

WEBB, SMITH, DOUGLAS & BEAUCHAMP   **June 1980-August 1983**
Houston, Texas

<u>Associate Attorney</u> with firm of thirty attorneys engaged in a general civil practice with emphasis on the representation of energy-related clients.   Concentration of practice included banking, real estate, securities and energy.

LEGAL EDUCATION

Juris Doctor, 1980
Southern Ivy University School of Law
Class Standing: Top 25%

Honors and Activities:

- Editor, Journal of Law Review, 1979-1980

- Author, Feature, "Federal Transportation Commerce Act--Unfair Methods of Competition," 45 Journal of Law Review 727 (1979).

- Author, Commentary, "Commerce Regulation Under the Transportation Deregulation Act," 45 Journal of Law Review 886 (1980).

- Recipient of the Journal of Law Review Award for Best Commentary of 1979-1980.

- Recipient of 1978-1979 National Lawyers' Club Scholarship.

- Member of The Magistrates, an organization of twelve students per class selected by the faculty on the basis of scholarship and leadership.

- Vice President of the SIU Student Bar Association, 1979-1980.

PREVIOUS EDUCATION

M.B.A. Southeastern University, 1976
Teaching Assistant and Instructor of Business Communications Undergraduate Course

B.A. Southeastern University, 1975
Three-Year Degree Program
Superior Studies Program

Name
Address
Phone Number

SUMMARY

Extensive business experience developed from close contact with leading executives from area companies in the furtherance of company objectives. Provided internal leadership in formulating policy, strategy, budgeting and marketing initiatives. Positions held required frequent interface with board members and senior staff from companies. Special skills also include:

- Project Management
- Business Development

- Community Relations
- Public Policy

PROFESSIONAL EXPERIENCE

CHARITIES SOUTH - Austin, TX   **1980 - 1995**
Vice President

Responsible for the management of an annual budget of $1.85 million, a staff of 28, and a volunteer structure of over 20,000 in an area wide resource development program that produced $425 million for community programs and services.

- Provided professional staff support to CEOs and senior management.

- Staffed the only combined effort of community cooperation in resource development between Dallas and Ft. Worth.

- Established community relations by expanding proactive programs like customer service support, employee assistance programs, and recognition programs on a local and national level.

- Developed an on-the-job training module for staff that resulted in the successful completion of a $40 million project in less than 9 months.

- Developed and directed corporate development program that annually provided 8-10% increases.

- Coordinated with community planning agency for development of program/agency audits and community needs assessments.

- Developed and negotitated contracts for staff services and consultation with five other divisions.

- Staffed multiple boards of directors and committees.

- Created a position for the organization in the face of changing legislation to be the only legally defined organization to manage a program that gave the organization control of marketing, planning, and resource distribution.

- Improved a national program that provided for recognition of Fortune 500 companies for their community involvement.

CHARITIES SOUTH - Austin, TX   **1977-1980**
Director

Planned, developed and staffed various processes in the areas of administration, training, special projects and policy development. Managed 26% of the resource development effort that provided $25 million. Provided for agency, media, and public relations. Managed 15 staff and 75 loaned executives.

- Developed corporate case presentation book that produced 12-16% annual increases in resource development production.

- Developed and implemented a wage/salary administration program.

- Co-chaired a multi-ethic task force that developed a community service program subsequently integrated into several agencies' programs.

- Analyzed and simplified organizational systems and procedures.

WORLD DISASTER RELIEF   **1970-1977**
Director

Responsible for disaster preparedness and relief efforts for 75 counties along the Texas Gulf Coast. Supervised and managed a professional and volunteer staff of up to 950 on various relief efforts. Directed programs on 18 major relief operations with expenditures of over $95 million.

- Established and directed the plan to provide relief efforts that included survey of needs, budget, staffing, financial management, supplies and staff support facilities.

- Prepared and managed both annual and project budgets.

- Provided services to a multi-cultural population.

- Developed and maintained liaison with federal, state, local and military officials to implement an effective, timely response to customer needs.

MILITARY SERVICE   **1966-1970**

Honorably discharged after forty-five months active duty. Served as an aircraft commander and instructor pilot in flight units in southeast Asia and the United States. Assignments included tour in the flight unit that supports the White House and the Pentagon.

COMMUNITY ACTIVITIES

Boy Scouts of America

- Serve as assistant scoutmaster and associate advisor to Order of the Arrow chapter.

- Member CrossTimbers District Committee, Boy Scouts of America.

- Chaired Steering Committee for community wide Friends of Scouting annual campaign that resulted in a 105% increase.

EDUCATION
University of Texas Arlington - Arlington, Texas

Name
Address
Phone Number

SUMMARY

A Corporate Administrative Assistant / Executive Secretary with extensive experience at the highest executive level. Major strengths in organization and detail, verbal and written communication skills, and all aspects of personalized travel arrangements. Exercises exceptional judgement and works independently. A well-organized, dependable professional who takes pride in her work.

PROFESSIONAL EXPERIENCE

Western Securities, Sacramento, CA   1968 - 1992
Fifth largest bank holding company in the United States, with assets in excess of $84 billion.

CORPORATE ADMINISTRATIVE ASSISTANT to Chairman of the Board and CEO   1981-1992
Performed full range of secretarial and administrative support; drafted and prepared correspondence; managed extensive domestic/international travel arrangements; maintained complex business/social calendar; screened/answered mail and telephone calls; handled personal bookkeeping/recordkeeping; supervised other executive secretaries.

- Developed and coordinated detailed domestic and international travel itinerary for CEO and provided all necessary information related to scheduled business appointments and social events, significantly improving executive's productivity.

- Managed, organized, and distributed the full range of incoming executive correspondence. Made decisions on destinations and actions required on most items, releasing CEO for more important activities.

- Created a form that executive used to track business expenses more efficiently, expediting preparation of a final summary and ultimate reimbursement.

- Skillfully coordinated and dealt with the resolution of as many as 25 executive level customer complaints per week. Made decisions on appropriate solutions and action required to resolve issues originally targeted at the CEO.

- Developed and provided executive a daily and weekly computerized summary of business and social appointments.

- Coordinated meetings and appointments which frequently included regulators and major corporate clients.

SENIOR SECRETARY, Fiduciary Services Group   1978-1981
Provided secretarial support to Division Heads of Trust Marketing and Trust Real Estate Management Divisions, along with officers of their staff.

- Completed payroll reporting and processing for 10-30 management employees with 100% accuracy.

- Easily handled a high volume of dictation work for head of Trust Real Estate Management Division, at levels up to 120 words per minute.

- Managed telephone contacts, correspondence, various reports, customer complaints, mail, meeting arrangements, and other appointments.

SECRETARY, Southern Division   1968-1978
Provided secretarial support to Regional Vice President, who supervised approximately 25 branches, along with other officers on his staff. Very heavy dictation and typing of internal memoranda and reports, handled customer complaints, mail, and telephones.

EDUCATION

Business
Pasadena City College, Pasadena, CA

Business - Diploma
Mary's Business High School, Buffalo, NY

PROFESSIONAL DEVELOPMENT

Glendale College, 1992
Lotus 1-2-3
Microsoft Windows 3.1
Advanced WordPerfect 5.1

SPECIAL SKILLS

WordPerfect 5.1
Typing - 60 wpm
Gregg Shorthand - 100 wpm
Dictaphone Capable

Name
Address
Phone Number

OBJECTIVE: Payroll Manager for retail or retail-support company

HIGHLIGHTS OF QUALIFICATIONS
- Eighteen years of progressive responsibility in the retail industry
- Reputation for dependability and credibility
- Strong commitment to cooperative teamwork
- Motivated to learn and grow in responsibility and business skills

1992 to present   PAYROLL MANAGER, Jones Department Stores
- Managed in-house system paying 7500 employees bi-weekly
- Supervised and evaluated 5 payroll and benefit clerks
- Monitored wage garnishments, tip and commission calculations
- Oversaw $19,000 annual supply and $150,000 annual staff payroll budget
- Responsible for timely deposits of payroll taxes using BankAmeritax
- Coordinated company-wide conversion to MSA-based payroll system
- Experience with Microsoft Excel, Word, LOTUS 123

1988 to 1992   REPLENISHMENT DIVISION MANAGER, Jones Department Stores
- Monitored, analyzed, updated computer-based order system for 40 vendors in 10 departments, generating $25 million in sales
- Supervised and evaluated 15 personnel in 4 states in special projects including counts, repricing, reticketing of 75 to 100 vendors
- Built effectiveness through better communication between stores and buyers

1985 to 1988   INVENTORY CONTROL MANAGER, Jones Department Stores
- Reduced shortage for 150,000 sq ft store from 3.5% of sales in July 1985 to 0.8% of sales in July 1988

1975 to 1988   Salesperson, Bridal Registrar, Assistant Department Manager, Receiving Dock Manager, Supply and Gift Wrap Manager - Jones Department Stores

EDUCATION   University of Windsor   Windsor MA   Liberal Arts

Name
Address
Phone Number

SUMMARY

A seasoned professional with 16 years experience in the management and administration of day-to-day operations in branch offices and administrative support units for a major organization. Major strengths in workflow production, research and problem solving, heavy customer service interaction, staffing and personnel administration, IRA and 401K administration, and general ledger accounting. A dependable, thorough and well organized planner with a successful track record in loss prevention, customer satisfaction and retention, increasing personnel morale and production, and technical expertise in audit and compliance regulations.

ACCOMPLISHMENTS

Workflow Production and Project Directing

- Developed and implemented operating procedures for the Retirement Plans Administration Unit, eliminating over $300,000 in overtime expense annually.

- Headed and administered all aspects of operations for a unit involving disbursements, new accounts, customer service, general accounting, research, and government reporting.

- Implemented and administered an accounting system for the unit, developing personalized general ledger accounts and a specialized cost center in order to identify all assets, liabilities, income and expense.

- Created and developed accounting and control procedures for the collection, remittance, balancing and year end reporting of tax withholding to the federal and state agencies.

- Increased productivity over 50% by formulating and administering the operational and audit criteria for an automated disbursement function, and on-line file system.

Research/Problem Solving and Loss Prevention

- Recovered 2.5MM in potential losses, and set up control procedures to avoid re-occurrence.

- Developed and enforced stringent audit procedures for the disbursements on IRA and KEOGH accounts for a $2.5 billion portfolio, thereby eliminating the possibility of losses and fraudulent activity.

- Alerted to unusual activity, uncovered and investigated fraudulent activity involving forgeries, saving the bank over $700,000 in losses.

- Transformed poor audit ratings and exceptions to a consistent "excellent rating" from 1980-1990.

- Researched, investigated, responded and administered all 1991 year end IRA reporting corrections within a 60 day period (meeting IRS deadlines) from over 650 banking offices - totaling over 950 corrections.

- Researched and responded with extensive supporting documentation to the IRS to dispel a 1987 and 1988 tax lien, saving the bank over $200,000.

<u>Customer Service</u>

- Upon centralization of major customer service areas, reduced the number of accounts requiring special handling by 75% through system improvements and customer negotiations.

- Achieved a 90% improvement in teller line "grid lock" by implementing new check cashing procedures on paydays.

- Won consistent recognition for the banking offices in accelerating quality customer service by resolving customer disputes and discrepancies in an expedient time frame.

<u>Team Building</u>

- Initiated monthly staff meetings and employee of the month awards, increasing staff morale, performance and involvement.

- Created and implemented cross selling techniques to an operations staff that increased banking office sales in loans, payroll, and trust services by 30%.

- Developed and conducted management meetings and seminars for exempt and non-exempt staff in the areas of affirmative action, EFT and other regulatory requirements, money laundering, safety in the workplace, handling the irate customer, United Way campaign, and introduction of all new operational procedures and new marketing products.

- Established and communicated expected standards of performance, reviewed actual performance, counseled, career coached, taking corrective action where necessary resulting in a cohesive department that delivered service effectively.

WORK HISTORY

National Bank, Los Angeles, CA	**1977 - Present**
<u>Retirement Plans Administration</u>, VP Operations	1990 - Present
<u>South Pasadena Office</u>, VP Operations	1988 - 1989
<u>Wilshire Grand Office</u>, VP Operations	1985 - 1988
<u>Headquarters Office</u>, AVP Operations, AVP Loans	1980 - 1985
<u>Various Branch Offices</u>, Assistant Manager	1977 - 1980

EDUCATION

Convent High School, Alhambra, California

Various business courses at East Los Angeles College, Pasadena City College, and Citrus College

Name
Address
Phone Number

SUMMARY STATEMENT

Diversified experience in the development, creation, and coordination of event sponsorships and literature; interfacing with outside advertising agencies and vendors. Strong interpersonal skills, communication skills, and computer literate.

EXPERIENCE

Sparkles Company, Modesto, CA   **1974 - 1994**

Assistant Marketing Manager

- Managed event sponsorships and charitable contributions. Program grew 25% per year in the number of events and contributions made. Resulted in increased brand name recognition, goodwill and public relations. Developed and maintained a system to track and monitor programs.

- Managed creative and fiscal relationships with various advertising agencies in the placement of telephone directory advertising ($700M budget, 350 directories) and free standing inserts ($950M budget) in six marketing areas.

- Participated in the development and promotion of new products and geographical expansion.

- Assisted in the development, creation, and management of brochures, sales pieces, promotional and informational literature.

- Created, developed, and followed process through distribution of 60 versions of delivery schedules annually to a customer base of 500,000 and within the organization.

- Coordinated the production, distribution, and shipment of billing inserts to stuffing/mailing houses for three brands with separate and unique billing cycles.

- Participated in the development of a new customer retention program, managed the ongoing fulfillment of the program, post implementation.

- Communicated new advertising/marketing materials to all public contact personnel through stand-up presentations and written material.

EDUCATION AND TRAINING

A.A. in Business Administration, San Bernardino Valley College. Graduated with Honors.

Completed 75% of course work towards B.S., Business, Cal Poly, Pomona:

- Public Relations
- Business and Creative Writing
- Advertising
- Computers

Dale Carnegie Institute - Effective Speaking and Human Relations Certificate

San Bernardino Valley College - Industrial Supervision Certificate

PROFESSIONAL AFFILIATIONS

Sparkles Company Employees Federal Credit Union - Board of Directors	1992 - Present
- Loan Committee Chairperson	1986 - 1992
Dale Carnegie Institute - Graduate Assistant	1988
Women in Management - Member	1981 - 1984

Name
Address
Phone Number

SUMMARY

Highly motivated and efficient individual with a strong background in accounting and office administration. Demonstrated analytical skills and attention to detail. Flexible in performance of job duties and effective team player

EXPERIENCE

WESTCO, Los Angeles, CA.   **1984 - Present**

<u>Savings Plan Assistant, Human Resources</u>   1992 - Present

- Coordinated over fifty new enrollments per month in the 401(k) plan, notified employees and started payroll deductions and validated transactions with the highest degree of accuracy.
- Identified and processed new hires age 40 and over for immediate enrollment
- Monitored new enrollments with prior 401(k) contributions and preserved the annual pre-tax contribution integrity.
- Processed all activities for terminated employees, sent required paperwork in timely manner.
- Notified Record Keeper and processed distributions, verified and distributed pay-outs.
- Handled inter-company transfers, received and sent 401(k) files, year-to-date contribution information to receiving company, did retroactive calculations, notified Record Keeper of security changes.
- Audited monthly and weekly reports from the Record Keeper and HRIS.
- Reconciled 401(k) loan and company contributions weekly and monthly reports that resulted in faster retrieval of discrepancies.
- Created and ran Information Expert mainframe reports by illuminating manual functions.
- Answered active/terminated participants' questions on balances, changes, enrollments, loans, withdrawals, distributions ensuring a clear understanding of 401(k) rules and regulations.
- Assisted Coordinator in special projects.

<u>Payroll Accountant, Financial Services</u>   1991 - 1992

<u>Senior Payroll Specialist, Financial Services</u>   1989 - 1991

<u>Payroll Specialist, Financial Services</u>   1984 - 1989

- Maintained payroll check stock.
- Reconciled 401(k) fund allocations, prepared wire transfers and 401(k) journal entries.
- Set-up bank routing number for ACH direct deposits with a high degree of accuracy.
- Handled bank reconciliation for confidential payroll.
- Coordinated moving expenses and W-2 corrections.
- Prepared SUI quarterly returns in timely manner by avoiding penalties.
- Created and ran Information Expert mainframe reports by illuminating manual functions.
- Coordinated special projects and assisted Payroll Manager.

CHILD CARE CENTER, Manhattan Beach, CA   1983-1984
<u>Office Manager</u>

- Maintained Accounts Receivable, Accounts Payable.
- Prepared biweekly manual payroll.
- Handled bank reconciliation.
- Prepared monthly Profit and Loss statement.
- Maintained General Office activities.

EDUCATION AND TRAINING

Glendale Community College, Glendale, CA
Accounting

Virginia Medical School, Richmond, VA
Registered Nurse

WESTCO SPONSORED COURSES

- Information Expert - mainframe report writing DBS (MSA)
- Microsoft Word
- Microsoft Excel
- Business Writing
- Interpersonal Styles

Name
Address
Phone Number

SUMMARY

More than 15 years experience as a Data Entry Operator in the financial services industry. Strengths include accuracy, speed and attention to detail. Typing speed 60 words per minute.

EXPERIENCE

FIRST BANK, Sacramento, CA   **1979 - 1994**

<u>Senior Clerical Specialist</u>, Glendale, CA 1992 - 1994
Responsible for processing redemption certificates and clearing outstanding items for aging.

- Processed up to 50 redemption items daily, ensuring that all certificates were canceled and forwarded to the Records Center.

- Monitored print-outs of previous day's work and identified/corrected errors ensuring accurate processing of batches each day.

- Reviewed aging reports for prior year's transaction, researched and cleared $76 million outstanding items in 50 accounts.

- Assumed all supervisory duties in the Manager's absence, trained 4 temporary employees on Sunstar accounting system. Created a "tally sheet" form, used to record and track completed and unprocessed work.

- Received merit award for outstanding performance and dedication.

<u>Senior Data Entry Technician</u> 1987 - 1992
Input bonds and coupons on IBM Bondmaster System; researched and resolved duplicate coupon problems, assisted with logging batches, checked unposted batches, made reversals and repays, assisted Team Leader as needed.

- Researched and corrected 200 rejected items each day.

- Demonstrated flexibility by working long overtime hours as needed while maintaining accuracy and efficiency.

- Tracked and assigned bond numbers, ensuring accurate sequential order before printing.

<u>Sub-Unit Supervisor</u> 1979 - 1987
Supervise eight to nine employees in the Stock Transfer Section.

- Input of stop transfers on DAC System, reconciliation of computer print-outs require corrections to be sent out on computer rejects.

PROFESSIONAL DEVELOPMENT
Banking on People 1971
Pre-Supervisory Workshop 1979
Labor Relations 1980

Name
Address
Phone Number

SUMMARY

Organized, detail oriented administrative professional with more than 10 years experience in finance and accounting. Dependable, innovative and efficient individual who communicates effectively. Able to work under supervision and performs well under pressure. Familiar with various accounting software and spreadsheets including: Lotus 1-2-3, Excel, Paynet Plus, Microsoft Word, MSA payroll, and ASK systems.

PROFESSIONAL EXPERIENCE

MICROSERVICES, Los Angeles, CA   **1985 - Present**

Payroll and Benefits Administrator   1988 - Present

Responsible for payroll and the administration of Savings Plan (401K), various life insurance policies, Flex Plan, company provided medical and dental plans, HMO medical plans and other benefits. These responsibilities included employee communication and training, interfacing with third party benefit providers, coordinating with payroll for optional payroll deductions and remittances of payments to vendors.

- Saved approximately $19,000 per year in overtime expense by establishing and coordinating interface between Paynet Plus and ASK.

- Processed biweekly payroll for as many as 700 employees using Paynet Plus software.

- Established comprehensive reconciliation processes for payroll accounts to book over $40,000 in salaries and other expenses. Accurately reconciled biweekly cash disbursements and various other payroll accounts.

- Streamlined method to record exceptions for hourly and salaried employees.

- Prepared monthly General Ledger and reconciliations for up to 55 accounts. Performed regular account reviews and produced monthly summary reports.

- Reduced the monthly account reconciliation summary report 90% by consolidating printout.

IRON INC., Hollywood, CA   1974 - 1984

<u>Assistant Manager</u>

- Performed and supervised all functions related to A/P, A/R and payroll.

- Prepared quarterly State and Federal tax returns.

SKILLS

Lotus 1-2-3, Real World, PROFS, MSA Payroll, Paynet Plus, Microsoft Excel, ASK, Microsoft Word

<u>Languages - Trilingual:</u> English - Fluent in oral and written communication
Spanish - Fluent in oral and written communication
Greek   - Fluent in oral skills

EDUCATION AND TRAINING

Associate of Arts, Business Administration - Illinois University
Payroll Practice and Management, Los Angeles Mission College

PROFESSIONAL AFFILIATIONS

American Payroll Association

Name
Address
Phone Number

QUALIFICATIONS SUMMARY

Twenty years of experience in operations/manufacturing management with two Fortune 500 companies. Background includes:

- New Plant Start-Ups
- Empowerment and Team Management
- Diversity Training
- New Product and Package Introduction
- Hazardous Waste Management
- High-Speed Equipment Technology

- Manning Reduction and Cost Improvements
- Union Contract Negotiations/Administration
- World Class Maintenance
- Corporate Quality Standards
- Distributor Relations
- Fixed and Variable Budget Preparation/Administration

PROFESSIONAL EXPERIENCE

BREWMEISTER COMPANY, Los Angeles, CA   **1975 - Present**

Modern high-speed facility producing 5.5 million barrels (171 million gallons) of beer per year with bottle line speeds up to 1100 units per minute and can line speeds up to 1600 units per minute.

Packaging Manager   **1989 - Present**

Report to Operations Manager. Responsible for overall department operations, directing activities of 36 salaried employees and 500 operators, with budget responsibility of $100+ million.

- On a continuous basis, streamlined operations through improved equipment reliability, operator development, realignment of job duties and reduction in work force resulting in saving of over $11 million over the last three years.

- Instituted Total Quality Management process resulting in record performance in corporate-administered internal compliance audits and a 30% reduction in scrap rates.

- Coordinated new product start-ups. All start-ups showed operational profit ahead of schedule.

- Planned and directed department Career Development Program, resulting in promotions or interdepartmental movement of over 50% of management staff in a three-and-a-half-year period.

- Implemented a World Class Maintenance Program resulting in a 15% reduction in maintenance out-of-service time and a 25% reduction in major line changeover times.

- Founding member of the Plant Cultural Diversity Task Team. Administered a $500,000 plant-wide Diversity Education Program.

- Coordinated efforts resulting in 50% reduction of solid waste to landfill and three-fold increase in revenues from sales of scrap.

- Developed the long-range master plan for the company's Packaging Operations which is projected to reduce costs corporation-wide by $91 million a year by the year 2000.

-2-

Distribution Manager   1984 - 1989

Responsible for plant production scheduling, material receiving, warehousing, shipping and traffic functions. Responsible for the activities of 24 salaried and 150 union employees.

- Installed new computerized distributor order handling system and truck control systems resulting in $600,000 in labor savings per year.

- Phased out all off-site warehouse storage through consolidation and reduction in finished goods inventory. Eliminate $700,000 in annual warehouse rental fees.

- Improved truck-loading efficiency from 11 trucks per person per shift, to 14 per shift through a series of procedural changes.

Brewery Services Manager   1982 - 1984

Responsible for combining the previously independent functions of Industrial Engineering, Production Control, Plant Sanitarian, Manpower Coordination and Cost Improvement. Supervised 20 management employees.

- Developed and administered $7.5 million in cost improvement capital spread across 60 projects in all departments. Minimum 25% return on investment achieved for all projects.

- Increased plant production capacity by 10% over a two-year period.

Quality Assurance Manager   1980 - 1982

Directed the activities of 30 salaried and 25 union laboratory workers. Coordinated the activities of the Microbiology Lab, analytical chemistry functions, packaging line quality monitoring, technical packaging (materials) and sensory evaluation.

- Managed the phased shut-down of laboratory functions in an old facility while simultaneously starting up operations in a new $250 million brewery.

- Reduced consumer complaint frequency by half, from the highest among the six plants to second lowest.

Unit Manager, Packaging Quality Control   1979 - 1980
Unit Manager, Product Quality Control   1977 - 1979
Quality Control Supervisor/Group Supervisor   1975 - 1977

USA BREWING COMPANY, Indianapolis, IN   **1972 - 1975**
Quality Control Manager
Quality Control Microbiologist
Quality Control Technician

EDUCATION AND TRAINING

Bachelor of Science, Biology, Melman University, Melman, Illinois

Lauhoff GMP Program
Juran's Management of Quality Seminar
Kaleel Jamison Managing Cultural Diversity Workshops
Kepner Tregore Problem Solving Seminar
Personnel Decisions, Inc., Leadership Program

Name
Address
Phone Number

EXECUTIVE SUMMARY

Public relations executive with proven ability in strategic planning, project management and mass communications. Strong background in translating corporate messages into appropriate communications media: publications, films, exhibits, entertainment and special events. Productive manager of community and media relations. Experienced in reporting for major news media and in directing the public relations function in non-profit, private and public companies.

Special expertise in:

- Entertainment Production

- Written and visual communications

- Creative special events and exhibits

PROFESSIONAL EXPERIENCE AND ACCOMPLISHMENTS

BEVERAGES, INCORPORATED - Dallas, Texas   **1988-1994**
Director of Corporate Communications

Directed public relations for nation's third largest soft drink company with staff of one communications specialist and two editors. Responsibilities included planning, budgeting, publications, media relations, special events, entertainment production, major exhibit management, and public relations activities to enhance the company's image with its publics.

- Directed development of a strategy to boost the company's support among Hispanics, generating strong national media coverage and on-going ties to Hispanic leaders.

- Recommended, booked and produced local and national entertainment acts including Natalie Cole, Reba McEntire, Vince Gill, Kenny Loggins and many others, all of which received standing ovations, creating a favorable impact on customer relations.

- Created and published an 86-page award-winning book, which has been reviewed favorably in newspapers across the country and ordered by more than 50,000 consumers.

- Directed the creation and operation of two major image-enhancing industry exhibits, effectively managing the million-dollar annual budget.

- Created and managed production on budget of a 15-minute film to introduce the corporation and industry to prospective employees and other audiences.

SODA, INC. - Houston, Texas   **1987-1988**
Director of Corporate Communications

Directed public relations function for Fizzie while closing the company's public affairs function in St. Louis and moving it to the Dallas headquarter of Dr. Salt Company.

THE AD AGENCY - Dallas, Texas   **1980-1987**
Dallas Bureau Chief

Managed news coverage of advertising and marketing activities in the Southwest for major marketing weekly published by Chicago-based Crane Communications.

MORNING NEWS - Houston, Texas   **1976-1980**
Business Writer

SOUTHERN UNIVERSITY - Houston, Texas   **1975-1976**
Full-time student in pursuit of Master of Fine Arts degree in Mass Communications.

XYZ RADIO - Amarillo, Texas   **1974**
Advertising Manager

MOUNTAIN REAL ESTATE - Houston, Texas   **1973**
Regional Advertising and Public Relations Manager for real estate developer.

DONALD ANDERBERG COMPANY - Houston, Texas   **1972-1973**
Director of Public Relations for regional commercial real estate operation.

SOUTHERN UNIVERSITY - Houston, Texas   **1969-1972**
Director of Communications for SMU School of Business.

ROBERTSON ASSOCIATES - Pittsburgh, Pennsylvania   **1965-1969**
Director of Communications for RMA (National Association of Bank Loan & Credit Officers).

US MILITARY   **1961-1965**
Following graduation from Officer Candidate School, served aboard USS MARLBOROUGH as Administrative Assistant to the Executive Officer, and as Public Information Officer.

EDUCATION

BA Economics, Southern Methodist University (1961)
MFA Mass Communications, Southern Methodist University (1981)

PROFESSIONAL AND COMMUNITY AFFILIATIONS

Public Relations Society of America (Member)
Meeting Professionals International (Member)
Business Associates Program, Cox School of Business, SMU (Mentor)

Name
Address
Phone Number

SUMMARY

Fifteen years of demonstrated experience in Protein Chemistry and Immunology. Designed novel immunotherapeutics. Initiated studies on cytokine control of lymphocyte differentiation with emphasis on receptor mediated cell development. Expertise in protein isolation, purification, characterization, and modification of proteins. Ability to conceptualize and integrate new areas of expertise into company framework. Successfully organized research staff into creative research teams.

EXPERIENCE

CONSULTANT   **1992 - Present**

Technical development of diagnostics and therapeutics.

PHARMACEUTICALS, INC., Burbank, CA   **1987 - 1992**
A liposome based pharmaceutical company
Senior Research Scientist

Developed liposome based anti-inflammatory therapeutics using biological response modifiers for the treatment of graft rejection, allergy, and rheumatoid arthritis. Experiments designed to follow efficacy of therapeutics in lymphocytes responsible for these immune disorders. Studies implemented to follow receptor driven control of drug delivery, efficacy and intracellular location of endocytosed drugs in T-cells and macrophages. Managed personnel responsible for experimental procedures on three projects. Worked with upper level management to maintain integration of projects within company's realm of activities. Prepared business plans, reports, and budgets for projects.

- Developed patentable technology for company.

- Developed an *in vitro* cell culture facility to monitor mechanism of action for pharmaceuticals under development.

- Expanded company's technology base by submitting proposals, receiving $94,000 from National Institute of Health (N.I.H.) for exploratory projects.

- Managed research contract in collaboration with international pharmaceutical company.

SMITTS CLINIC RESEARCH INSTITUTE, Baltimore, MD   **1983 - 1987**
RICHARDS MEDICAL COLLEGE, New York, NY
Research Associate

Investigated the mechanism of cytolytic T-cell killing of target cells. Purification, characterization, and identification of cytolytic granule proteins involved in target cell lysis. Preparation of LAK cells for clinical trials of IL-2 therapy in cancer patients.

-2-

UNIVERSITY OF ANYTOWN
<u>Research Fellow</u>   **1982 - 1983**

Introduced recombinant DNA techniques to the group and initiated cloning the SDH gene from somatic cell hybrid.

<u>Postdoctoral Research Physicist</u>   **1980 - 1981**

Studies on the retinal rod disk membrane structure, proteins using chemical cross-linking methodology.

IVY UNIVERSITY   **1977 - 1980**
<u>N.I.H. Postdoctoral Fellow</u>

Investigated the oligomeric structure of the sarcoplasmic reticulum membrane ATPase using chemical cross-linking methodology. Developed deuterium - sucrose gradients to quantitate protein concentration in reconstituted membrane vesicles.

EDUCATION AND TRAINING

Ph.D. in Biochemistry
State University of New York at Stony Brook, 1976

A.B. Biochemistry, Minor in English Literature
University of California at Berkeley, 1968

Bilingual: Second Language - French.

HONORS

Recipient, S.B.I.R. Grant, NIH/NIAID, 1991-1992

Recipient, S.B.I.R. Grant, NIH/NIMSD, 1991-1992

N.I.H. Post Doctoral Fellow, 1976-1980

Name
Address
Phone Number

SUMMARY

Experienced geophysical interpreter/explorationist, a proven oil finder, specializing in creative and innovative concepts in prospect generation and evaluation in both the International and United States petroleum industry. Strong interpretational skills in seismic stratigraphy and structural geology with the ability to evaluate large data bases quickly. Excellent team player with strong communication and problem solving qualities.

PROFESSIONAL EXPERIENCE

MAXIMUM ENERGY INC.   **1989-1994**
Senior Exploration Advisor

- Evaluated basins and plays resulting in acreage acquisitions and drilling commitments with expenditures ranging from 3 to 30 million dollars.

- Assembled and interpreted large geophysical and geologic data bases resulting in recommendations for acreage acquisitions and exploratory work programs in International Bid Rounds.

- Utilized a multidisciplinary approach to assess the hydrocarbon potential of basins in over 40 countries, with focus areas in South America, CIS, North Africa and Eastern Europe.

- Planned, managed a $500,000 budget, and supervised a multinational exploration team.

AMERICAN GAS & OIL   **1988-1989**
Principal Research Geologist

- Performed regional geologic and seismic interpretation of the North Slope, Alaska leading to the proposed drilling of 2-4 wells.

- Evaluated portions of the East Java Sea, Indonesia, resulting in a gas discovery in the Kangean Island Area.

- Assessed the potential of the Taranaki Basin of New Zealand resulting in acreage acquisition and drilling commitments.

ABC CONSULTANTS   **1985 - 1988**
Consulting

- Performed regional evaluation of the Sacramento Basin, California, resulting in the identification of over twenty prospects and four gas discoveries.

- Evaluated plays in the Big Horn Basin, Wyoming and the Smackover trend of Florida resulting in prospect identification and acreage acquisitions.

PROFESSIONAL EXPERIENCE (continued)

- Conducted a multidisciplinary evaluation of the Circum-North Atlantic focusing on SE Greenland and Portugal.

PETROLEUM USA   **1979-1985**
Division Geophysicist

- Performed interpretation resulting in discoveries totaling approximately 75 million barrels of oil equivalent both in the Gulf Coast and Rocky Mountain Regions.

- Developed and managed geophysical budgets ranging up to 5 million dollars.

- Coordinated seismic contractors and processors in the acquisition, processing, and modeling of seismic data.

- Supervised technical staff of 10 geophysicists and support personnel.

SOUTHERN OIL COMPANY   **1976-1979**
District Geophysicist

- Conducted interpretations leading to discoveries totaling approximately 25 million barrels of oil equivalent in the Lower Wilcox-Midway trend of south Texas.

- Developed and managed a 3 million dollar annual geophysical budget.

- Coordinated seismic contractors and processors in the acquisition and processing of seismic data.

OIL AMERICA   **1964-1976**
Senior Petroleum Geophysicist

- Assisted in the confirmation and delineation of the giant Prudhoe Bay Field, Alaska.

- Performed interpretation resulting in discoveries totaling over 500 million barrels of oil in the Endicott, Point Thompson, and Flaxman Island areas of the North Slope, Alaska.

- Conducted evaluations of the Haynesville Limestone Trend of East Texas resulting in discoveries along the western edge of the Sabine Uplift.

- Performed regional and seismic stratigraphic facies analyses for the evaluations of offshore lease sales resulting in acreage acquisitions and drilling commitments with expenditures exceeding 50 million dollars.

EDUCATION

M.S., Geology, University of Arkansas, 1965
B.S., Geology, University of Arkansas, 1963

Name
Address
Phone Number

OBJECTIVE

Senior operations or staff management position in the specialty retail or service industry.

SUMMARY

Management professional with proven success in operations and staff management effectively utilizing participative management and team building skills. Managed multiple high volume, fast pace, retail operating units comprised of franchised and corporate stores to record performances. Managed the development and implementation of the largest electronic point-of-sale project in the convenience store industry. Experience includes:

- Franchise Operations
- Sales/Marketing
- Purchasing/Distribution
- Fiscal Management
- Corporate Operations
- Automated Systems

PROFESSIONAL EXPERIENCE

THE SOUTH COMPANY   **1974 - 1993**
South Stores, the leading convenience retailer and gasoline marketer recording sales in excess of $8 billion. The company operates 5,600 franchised and corporate stores in the United States and Canada. Licensees world-wide.

Market Manager - Dallas, Texas   **1992 - 1993**
Total operational responsibility for Dallas based market supporting 71 corporate operated stores. Profit and loss responsibility for annual market revenues in excess of $95 million. Directed the activities of market staff members and approximately 700 store level personnel.

- Developed a strong sense of team throughout the market establishing a quality communications process.

- Built most positive sales trend in the Dallas/Ft. Worth market area.

- Coordinated the development of professional staff's qualifications for promotional opportunities.

- Executed asset management procedures which produced a 40% reduction in inventory losses.

- Coached quality customer service practices reducing customer complaints.

- Empowered field staff to make decisions improving and streamlining the daily flow of business.

- Exceeded prior year's operating profits in excess of 55%.

Manager - Stores Automation - Dallas, Texas   **1983 - 1992**
Managed the development process under the review of Chief Operating Officer resulting in the definition of Southland's strategic retail automation strategy.

- Directed the development of long range automation strategies resulting in $60 million in capital expenditures; $12 million in annual operating expenses. Provided advice and counsel to senior executives including Chairman, President, CFO, and COO.

- Established and managed co-development relations with system vendor, guiding development of hardware and software unique to the company's needs. Negotiated purchase agreement of 7,000 store systems.

- System installation generated immediate labor savings of 3 to 4.5% per month per store.

- Developed ongoing field support options resulting in savings of $1.9 million annually.

- Improved expense controls and productivity during every budget cycle.

Franchise Analysis Manager - Dallas, Texas   **1982 - 1983**
Managed and developed the resources necessary to evaluate and update our franchise offering.

- Improved the marketability of the company's franchise offering versus all other franchisers nationwide.

- Led management action group which improved franchise operations by centralizing management and communications functions.

- Improved efficiency and overall sales of franchise operations by leading the development of standardized operations review.

- Initiated the development of franchise equity building program which reduced franchisee debt and improved cash flow.

Zone Manager - Store Operations - San Jose, CA   **1978 - 1982**
Full management responsibility for California based zone comprising 96 franchised and corporate run stores. Managed headquarters and field staff of 140. Full P&L responsibility for three districts with total revenue of $65 million. Developed a sense of "team" in zone employees and of consistency in the franchise community.

- Built per store sales and overall zone profitability to highest in the entire division.

- Generated growth, leading construction of six new stores and sale of 25 new franchises.

- Recruited, selected, and developed three new district managers, and guided development of 25 field representatives.

- Reduced shortage by mandating strict implementation of corporate loss prevention program in all zone locations.

- Lowered franchisee turnover by increasing level and frequency of direct contact and promoting goodwill through communications, support, and follow through.

District Manager - Santa Cruz, CA   **1977 - 1978**

Field Representative - Sacramento, CA   **1974 - 1977**

EDUCATION

B.A., Business Administration
Hastings College
Hastings, New York

Name
Address
Telephone

SUMMARY

Executive with over 15 years of increasing responsibility in retail management and the ability to operate effectively in a transitional environment. Notable skills/achievements have included streamlining operations and developing successful cost-cutting measures. Excellent interpersonal skills.

Areas of expertise:

- Operations Management
- Budget Preparation
- Real Estate

- Personnel Management
- Merchandising
- Loss Prevention

PROFESSIONAL EXPERIENCE

FISHER STORES - Houston, Texas   **1983-Present**

Senior Vice President, Store Operations 1994-Present
Full responsibility for operations management and P&L for a $190 million general merchandise company with 163 stores.

- Reorganized regional and district manager staff, resulting in a $140K annual savings while improving district coverage.

- Reduced store payroll costs by redesigning payroll guidelines and formulas, resulting in a $1.3 million annual savings.

- Implemented a store loss-prevention and safety audit, resulting in 70% accident reduction and $300K per year savings in claims and premiums.

- Converted and integrated 60 acquired stores to Fisher format within 90-day timetable.

- Reduced annual budget by 30% in the Loss Prevention Department through implementing several cost-saving measures with no loss in coverage.

- Streamlined store supply department, resulting in 40% reduction of forms and products -- an annual savings of $200K.

- Improved store-wide ordering system that allowed transportation to realign delivery routes, resulting in a savings of $250K annually.

<u>Vice President, Store Operations</u> 1987-1994
Responsible for direction and full P&L of entire store operations, with sales of $130 million including sales, inventory, payroll forecasts and budgets for 104 stores, planning and implementation of store advertising, and merchandising strategies.

* Developed an S.O.P. (Standard Operating Procedure) for all stores, resulting in clarification of operating procedures and consistency throughout the chain.

* Initiated the development of a manager recruiting program that resulted in the hiring of 11 manager trainees during a difficult hiring economy. (All were subsequently promoted to manager status.)

* Implemented automotive coordinator position, which resulted in improved automotive orders and 15% sales increase with a 20% reduction in inventory.

* Developed and promoted 4 regional managers and 15 district managers.

<u>Regional Manager</u> 1983-1987
Responsible for operation of 60 stores and 7 district managers with sales of $78 million, including sales and profit forecasting, expense control, implementation of merchandising, advertising strategies, and inventory control.

* Developed and promoted 4 district managers and 32 store managers.

* Averaged 19% comparable store increases in 1985.

* Opened 22 new stores in 1985.

<u>EDUCATION</u>

Associate in Arts, Houston College

Several Management Seminars

<u>SPECIAL ACCOMPLISHMENTS</u>

Chairman of Rehabilitation Center Annual Fund Drive (raised $160K)

Name
Address
Phone Number

SUMMARY

Diversified experience in marketing, advertising, pricing, promotion and sales analysis. An "entrepreneur" who stimulates team creativity and focuses resources on key objectives. Exceptional analytical, strategic planning and negotiation skills complemented by strong "hands on" knowledge of media and creative production.

PROFESSIONAL BACKGROUND

NATIONAL EYEWEAR - Houston, Texas   **1994 - 1995**
<u>Vice President, Marketing</u>

Led a department of 12 persons and four agencies in the planning and execution of a $41 million annual marketing plan encompassing advertising, media, promotion and field marketing.

- Developed the "Trusted Leader" advertising campaign that positioned the company as having a track record of better quality than other chain competitors.

- Generated the company's first ever motion picture tie-in promotion.

- Secured national exposure by negotiating a four minute "eyewear fashion" story on "Main Floor", a syndicated television magazine following Good Morning America.

- Streamlined the print planning process to reduce time and costs by 30%.

BURGERWORLD - Los Angeles, California   **1986 -1994**
<u>Vice President, Field Marketing & Promotion</u>

Responsible for development of marketing programs and media plans on the local, regional and national level.

- Led a department of 18 persons and directed or influenced a $54 million annual marketing budget. System sales were $1.1 billion through 800 company-owned and 400 franchised locations.

- Made significant contributions to achieving over a 90% increase in system sales since 1986. This included unit expansion of almost 500 restaurants and a number of quarters with double digit same store sales increases.

- Supervised the development of marketing plans for entry into new markets resulting in record breaking opening sales.

- Initiated a change in the Franchise Contract increasing the Marketing Contribution from 4% to 5% which resulted in an increase of $8 million per year in marketing resources.

- Turned a cost center for field and franchise local support materials into a profit center with over a $100K contribution to overhead.

- Created a sales building culture in the organization through the development of a Local Marketing Workshop, a new marketing manual, a "Marketer of the Year" recognition program and a user friendly materials ordering system.

- Created and executed a regional promotion strategy that generated an additional $5-7 million in additional media exposure each year.

- Developed an "internal customer focused" department that helped to maintain a productive and open relationship with franchisees.

- Served as the primary contact for existing and prospective international franchisees.

- Developed tie-in promotions with Home Alone II, Dennis the Menace, Star Trek Generations and other motion picture releases.

GENERAL CONSULTANTS - Burbank, California   **1986**
<u>Vice President</u>

Provided promotion consulting services for Hardee's Restaurants, New World Entertainment, Coca Cola and various retail clients.

ACE ADVERTISING - Monterey, California   **1985 - 1986**
<u>Account Supervisor</u>

Managed the sales promotion and field marketing functions for the JACK IN THE BOX account.

BURGERWORLD - Santa Monica, California   **1982 - 1985**
<u>Zone Marketing Manager</u> - Los Angeles, Hawaii

FAST FOOD INC. - Costa Mesa, California   **1981 - 1982**
<u>Area Marketing Manager</u> - Los Angeles, Hawaii

PEPPERONI CITY - Amsterdam, New York   **1979 - 1981**
<u>Regional Marketing Manager</u> - New York, New England

COUGLIN ASSOCIATES ADVERTISING, Hollywood, California   **1978 - 1979**
<u>Account Executive</u>

Serviced Kentucky Fried Chicken advertising cooperatives in Southern California, South Florida and San Antonio.

NEW HORIZONS ADVERTISING - Hudson, New York   **1975 - 1978**
<u>President</u>

Ran an advertising agency with accounts that included Night Clubs, the Mystic Mt. Ski Resort, musical groups, restaurants, a toy store and a telephone retailer. Handled all facets of advertising agency operations including media buying, copywriting, art direction, production and client service.

THE FILM COMPANY - New York, New York   **1975**
<u>Production Assistant/Reader</u>

EDUCATION

Harvard Business School, Strategic Marketing Management, 1991
SUNY Buffalo BS, Business Marketing/Finance, 1975
New York University Institute of Film and Television, 1974

Name
Address
Phone Number

SUMMARY

Energetic leader with seven years of strategic marketing and project management experience for both business and consumer markets. Experience includes strategic planning, market analysis, research, distribution, pricing, vendor relations, product management and implementation. Proven record of success in technical, service-oriented businesses.

EXPERIENCE

AIR USA, Dallas, Texas   **1991 - 1995**

Manager, Product Distribution   *1993 - 1995*
Directed research of options for future distribution strategies, enhancement of systems to support new and existing technology and day-to-day maintenance of current channels. Led staff of up to 12 management employees.

- Restructured staff responsibilities to improve productivity and customer and vendor relationships. Reorganized individuals onto teams with like responsibilities and assigned team leaders. Group productivity improved 20%.

- Determined appropriate level of company participation in vendor products to maximize marketing distribution benefits. Led analyses of revenue benefits; saved $15 million in startup costs and $12 million in ongoing fees.

- Directed research and analyses to isolate more profitable methods of categorizing fare products. Identified and implemented changes; improved revenue by $8 million annually.

- Directed design and implementation of enhancements to restrict abuse of inventory. Increased revenue by $25 million annually.

- Led interdepartmental project to develop new airport passenger processing procedures and systems. Directed 15 managers to prepare proposal, system development plans and procedural enhancements, analyze profitability and create a Board presentation. Proposal approved; projected savings of $17 million in first year.

Senior Market Analyst   *1992-1993*
Led a team of five management employees to identify and implement marketing and pricing strategies.

- Analyzed market trends, implemented aggressive distribution changes and revised promotion and inventory management strategies to encourage booking of low volume flights. Increased revenue by $10 million annually and led underperforming markets to profitability.

- Analyzed expansion of transborder service. Evaluated critical market factors, determined profitability, demand trends and optimal aircraft types and configurations. Recommended phased implementation approach to minimize risk and maximize profitability.

- Initiated unique fare pricing to stimulate demand during an unusually low performing period. Analyzed seasonal trends, competitive pricing actions and overall market profitability. Launched sale in selected markets to prevent retaliatory competitive action. Grew demand by 20% and maintained profitability.

Senior Market Analyst (continued)   *1992-1993*

♦   Negotiated funding, acquired resources and directed five month development effort to launch new business class service for narrow body aircraft. Project implemented on time and within budget.

Market Analyst   *1991-1992*
Identified and implemented marketing and pricing strategies.

♦   Developed and implemented systematic change to ensure integrity of prices. Negotiated compliance across more than fifteen impacted departments. Improved revenue by $15 million.

US COMPUTERS, Modesto, California   **1990-1991**

Marketing Specialist
Ensured accurate positioning of new products in the Kindergarten through 12th grade (K-12) education marketplace.

♦   Directed the production of collateral materials for new product launch. Created video demonstrating product positioning for targeted market segments, wrote script for TV question/answer video, conducted user focus groups. Materials completed and implemented on time.

STUDENT LOAN CORPORATION, Boston, Massachusetts   **1986-1989**

Project Manager
Managed systems development for a start-up student loan company.

♦   Managed conversion from manual to automated processing for a $35 million loan portfolio. Coordinated work of over 30 users and programmers, wrote specifications and designed implementation plans. Decreased response time of customer service inquiries by 50% and grew portfolio by 45%.

♦   Developed and implemented new loan product. Analyzed costs, developed project plan, loan process flow and automation plans. Improved processing efficiency and reduced loan turnaround time by over 50%.

AWARDS

Who's Who Among Students in American Colleges and Universities   1985
Who's Who Among International Business Professionals   1995

EDUCATION

Anderson Graduate School of Management at UCLA, Los Angeles, **MBA, Marketing**   1991
Allegheny College, Meadville, Pennsylvania, **BS Math**   1986

Name
Address
Phone Number

SUMMARY

Resourceful, results-oriented manager with a record of achievement in all phases of marketing and sales of service to businesses in retail, health care, hospitality, direct marketing and various other arenas. Adept at identifying opportunities with strong profit potential--whether developing new business or turning around an existing business-devising strategies and organizing resources to exploit that potential, then taking or directing whatever actions are needed to maximize success.

A skilled negotiator and closer who is comfortable discussing multimillion dollar contracts with senior-level executives of the businesses' most important, most demanding or most sensitive customers.

A strong communicator capable of maintaining client relationships, managing diverse project teams and motivating subordinates.

PROFESSIONAL EXPERIENCE

CONNORS CONSULTING, Austin, Texas   **1992 - Present**

Sales/Sales Support Manager
New Business Development with companies that are industry leaders. Project Management including due diligence and transition projects as well as revenue engagements for existing clients. Managed the project teams as well as personnel that reported to me on a full time basis. Relationship building with senior level executives.

- Implemented a new sales methodology to better qualify potential opportunities and better manage limited resources to pursue those opportunities with best chance of closure.

- Successfully assisted in the signing of outsourcing contracts with the largest airline catering company and the largest reinsurance broker in the United States. Revenue from these contracts will total approximately $52 million over five years.

THE BUSINESS SERVICE COMPANY, Houston, Texas   **1990 - 1992**

National Account Manager
Marketing Research and Business Plan Development. New Business Development and Project and Major Account Management.

- Identified two target industries for products of the nation's largest electronic, point-of-sale services company.

- Developed and implemented appropriate marketing strategies for each of the target industries.

- Successfully marketed services to health care and fast food industry clients with revenues worth over $10 million.

- Guided the development and implementation of the clients that were brought in, and managed their ongoing operations.

BANKFIRST, Stamford, Connecticut   **1988 - 1990**

<u>National Marketing Manager</u>

<u>National Marketing Representative</u>

New Business development and major account management. Sales management responsibilities, and management of outside Sales Organizations that sold the banks merchant processing services.

- Implemented marketing and administrative strategies resulting in the turnaround of a national sales unit from $1 million in losses annually to profitability and expansion.

- Signed new business representing more than $630 million in processing volume, about $12.5 million in revenues.

<u>EDUCATION</u>

Masters of Business Administration, Thompson University
Madison, New Jersey

Bachelor of Science, Business Administration, Michael's College
Windham, Vermont
Magna Cum Laude

Name
Address
Phone Number

OBJECTIVE

Seeking a marketing or business manager position in which I can utilize my extensive management skills, marketing experience, and leadership abilities to significantly impact the success of a progressive, customer focused organization.

SUMMARY

A business professional possessing extensive marketing management and business development experience with a $700 million medical products manufacturer. Exceptional analytical, strategic planning, problem solving and negotiation skills. An effective communicator and leader with a broad professional background blending marketing, sales, manufacturing, and technical management experience.

- Technology/Product Licensing
- Acquisition Evaluation
- Global Product Management

- Strategic Planning
- Contract Negotiation
- Product Development

- Sales/Corporate Training
- Business Process Facilitator
- Total Quality Management

EXPERIENCE

MAJOR MEDICAL COMPANY - Kansas City, Missouri   **1983 - 1994**
A Fortune 200 medical products manufacturer of pharmaceuticals, medical devices and equipment for the Radiology, Cardiology, Nuclear Medicine, Anesthesiology and Critical Care markets.

Group Market Development Manager   1991 - 1994
Recruited by senior management to conduct market opportunity assessments for patented technology and to direct the corporate Business Process Quality Management project. Evaluated new product lines and acquisitions. Developed business proposals and negotiated license agreements. Integrated business processes for new product acquisitions.

- Commercialized patented drug delivery technology, including market assessment, business plan development and licensee identification, resulting in two multi-million dollar royalty agreements and a new business platform for the corporation.

- Negotiated and implemented three distributor agreements. Coordinated and managed multiple distributor relationships that complimented the core, direct selling business, resulting in expanding sales potential and increasing contract proposals by 20% (approximately $18 million in new business).

- Led the global marketing and manufacturing teams of a $45 million product line and developed a long range plan to out-source critical raw materials and reduce total product costs by 30% (approximately $7 million).

- Designed, implemented and directed a corporate Business Quality Process Management system. Trained divisional management and staff and facilitated four improvement projects which were expanded into a company wide reengineering effort estimated to reduce costs by $85 million.

- Facilitated the global product development team of a core $600 million product line which resulted in approval of a five year development plan to reduce total product cost by 28% (approximately $55 million).

Senior Marketing Manager
1989 - 1991

Managed two pharmaceutical and two medical device product lines ranging in annual sales of $6 to $80 million. Hired, trained and supervised a three-member marketing staff. Managed a marketing expense budget of $1.2 million.

- Created sales promotion involving a license agreement with a medical equipment manufacturer, more than doubling equipment sales and tripling pharmaceutical sales to $80 million in the second year of the promotion.

- Designed and implemented effective sales promotions involving physician peer selling, drug sampling and hospital equipment financing. Developed all supporting sales materials and trained the sales force.

- Recruited by senior management to lead an interdepartmental, 18 member, product development team and an eight member manufacturing team in resolving developmental and manufacturing issues and reversing an FDA non-approvable, obtaining market approval within 10 months of plan for an innovative drug delivery system.

- Developed, implemented, and managed the market launch of a new drug delivery system resulting in a 30% increase in sales, to $460 million, of a core product line.

- Directed the product development and facilitated the international market launches in Germany and Japan of an innovative drug delivery device working with international marketing teams and distributors.

Market Manager
1987 - 1989

Promotion without change of scope or market responsibility.

Product Manager
1985 - 1987

Accountable for all facets of product management including, market research, market analysis, strategic planning, product positioning, pricing, promotion, advertising, sales and production forecasting, expense budgeting and clinical studies.

- Recruited by senior management to conduct the market analysis of a $6 million, mature product line. Recommended divestiture, identified purchase candidates, assisted in the sales negotiation and led the sales transition team to transfer technology to acquiring company exceeding contract expectations.

- Managed $35 million, mature line of imaging agents. Maintained market share and margin in declining market environment by developing and implementing a unique differentiation strategy.

- Analyzed product costs after implementation of an activity based costing system and developed a new pricing strategy which resulted in taking advantage of short term high volume/low margin market opportunities, increased revenue by $3 million while maintaining incremental profitability.

Senior Market Research Analyst
1984 - 1985

Promotion without change of scope or market responsibility.

Market Research Analyst
1983 - 1984

Conducted marketing studies and analysis in all phases of marketing research including primary, secondary, new product concept and advertising research. Earned recognition from marketing management for developing sales forecasting models and reporting system.

MIDWEST CHEMICAL, INC. - Kansas City, Missouri
1980 - 1983

Quality Audit Supervisor

Hired, trained and supervised quality auditing department. Audited all drug manufacturing processes for conformance to federal drug manufacturing regulations. Interpreted federal register CGMP guidelines, developed and implemented auditing policy and procedures.

BEAUTY SUPPLIES - Kansas City, Missouri   **1977 - 1980**
Production Supervisor
Supervised thirty union production workers and technical staff in national brand, consumer products manufacturing facility. Represented management in labor relations and grievance committee actions.

PHARMACO - Kansas City, Missouri   **1974 - 1977**
Analytical Chemist
Performed chemical analysis and physical testing on raw materials, in-process work and finished products for specialty pharmaceutical manufacturer.

MIDWEST DISTRIBUTING - Kansas City, Missouri   **1971 - 1974**
Sales Representative
Expanded sales territory of local distributor selling consumer products to the retail trade. Achieved sales budgets and developed 120 new accounts resulting in over $400K of new business.

EDUCATION

M.B.A., Campbell College, Charles, Rhode Island	1983
B.S., Chemistry, University of Missouri - St. Louis, St. Louis, Missouri	1975
American Management Association, Financial Management	1994
University of Michigan School of Business, Marketing Management	1989

PROFESSIONAL ORGANIZATIONS

American Management Association
American Healthcare Radiology Administrators
American Marketing Association
Medical Marketing Association
Licensing Executives Society

Name
Address
Phone Number

SUMMARY

Twelve years of professional sales experience as an individual contributor and as a sales manager. A creative problem solver with excellent skills in consultative selling, key account sales, team building, strategic planning and training. Able to work and manage effectively in an environment of change. Confident and productive salesperson with strong leadership qualities.

PROFESSIONAL EXPERIENCE

FAIRLEIGH INCORPORATED, Bethel, New York   **1986 - 1995**

National Accounts Manager/OEM Sales   1993 - 1995

- Selected as National Accounts Manager to establish and maintain relationships with large national laboratory chains and key accounts. New National Account sales added 20% to plant volume during time of increasing overhead due to declining volume.

- Planned business direction as part of 4 member world-wide strategy team, to slow revenues erosion, implementing aggressive new approach and maintaining sales during a 20% market decline.

- Created telemarketing scripts for use by Customer Service, leading to attainment of annual sales goals before the end of the third quarter, even though head count decreased 33%.

Western Regional Sales Manager, Advanced Diagnostics Division   1991 - 1993

- Appointed Western Regional Sales Manager (33 states) for a new division and built a sales team from peers and former supervisor. Leadership, cooperative problem solving and focus on consultative selling led to the top two individual sales awards for the division.

- Coached sales representatives in territory management and prioritization of accounts, resulting in no per capita increase in expense despite doubling of territory sizes.

- Managed key accounts when the major product line was recalled and the field sales force was terminated, effectively maintaining our core business and preserving corporate image under extreme circumstances.

Senior Immunodiagnostic Specialist, Diagnostic Instrument Systems Division   1986 - 1991

- Managed a territory that had been vacant for 15 months and was the least productive in the U.S., bringing it to the top 20% in three years.

- Chosen as member of the Sales Training Development Team, writing, implementing, and delivering a comprehensive 8 week training program for new representatives.

- Served on the Marketing Launch Team for new $40,000 product. Designed marketing program, developed sales aids and implemented training for 22 representatives at launch.

BIO LABS, Brookline, MA   **1984 - 1986**
A manufacturer and distributor of cell cultures.

Account Executive

- Recruited at inception of new product to establish and expand business. Involved in creation of Technical and Customer Service operations. Formulated and implemented marketing plans.

CENTRAL LAB, Fairfax, VA   **1983 - 1984**
Supplier of cell culture media and EIA instrumentation.

Systems Specialist

- Brought territory to over 100% from 75% of goal, with running rate of $1.2 MM. Award for highest media sales for 1984. Field trained new representatives within 6 months of hire.

ADDITIONAL EXPERIENCE

- Directed QA lab for device manufacturer. Developed procedures, wrote QA specs, created Tech Service. Hired, trained and supervised lab and inspection personnel.

- Implemented NIH grant in Medical School laboratory. Set up, staffed, supervised all basic research efforts for the departmental laboratories.

EDUCATION

B.S., Biology, University of Maryland

AWARDS

President's Club, three years
Regional Representative of the Year

Name
Address
Phone Number

SUMMARY

Over 18 years as a professional with solid sales results, consistently making and exceeding goals. Prospect, qualify and close deals while maintaining a quality customer service relationship. Detail orientated and proficient at follow up and follow through.

ACCOMPLISHMENTS

CREDIT INCORPORATED

1980 - Present

<u>Senior Territory Manager</u>

Responsible for the development and maintenance of an establishment/merchant network in the Los Angeles County market.

- Expanded territory from Los Angeles to 13 Southern and Central California counties.

- Finished in the top 30% of the national sales force, annually.

- Recognized with bonus incentives for signing the most top holdouts in region.

- Achieved recognition as a repeat winner of President's Club.

- Increased new customer ability to use service by decreasing processing time 50%. Received special recognition for implementation of suggestion that facilitated use of service.

- Signed 30 restaurants in one month, exceeding goal by 100%.

- Increased restaurant coverage from 65% to 76% in territory.

- Signed top "gold" account for two consecutive years.

- Signed over 300 restaurants per year.

BUSINESS SYSTEMS INC.   **1978 - 1980**
<u>Sales Representative</u>

Sold business systems to a wide variety of organizations.

EDUCATION

B.F.A., Communication Arts, New York Institute of Technology.

Name
Address
Phone Number

SUMMARY

Sales and marketing executive with extensive direct and indirect sales experience resulting in consistent revenue overachievement and sales leadership. Expertise in problem analysis and resolution, sales strategies, new account development, account management and teaming for a wide variety of industries including Energy, Telecommunications, Aerospace, Medical, Manufacturing.

SIGNIFICANT ACCOMPLISHMENTS

- Four (4) years over 100% quota for district managers
- Two (2) years over 100% quota for branch managers
- Promotion of ten (10) people to sales management, eight (8) to sales executive
- Management and sales in excess of 800 million dollars in a variety of industries
- Eleven (11) years over 100% quota
- Seven (7) years in top 10% of corporation's sales force

EXPERIENCE

COMPUTER EQUIPMENT INCORPORATED   1978 - 1994
$2 billion full service computer company

HIGH PERFORMANCE COMPUTING SALES MANAGER   1992 - 1994
Responsible for the sales of high performance computing products in a client/server environment with Unix based software.
- Achieved 462% quota 1994, 129% quota 1993.
- Directed development of high performance computing business and sales plan.
- Created business plan and sales strategy for client/server computing.
- Consulted with major account teams on effective sales strategies to win strategic opportunities.
- Developed and expanded the use of the Sales Opportunity Management Tool by the sales force.
- **Supported creation of the Computer Equipment service plan.**
- Conceived and conducted high performance computing sales training.

NATIONAL ACCOUNTS SALES MANAGER   1989 - 1991
INDUSTRY ACCOUNTS, U.S. TERRITORY
Full profit and loss responsibility for all national accounts in the oil, gas, metals and glass industry.
- Led all Sales Managers in portfolio accounts, achieving in excess of 130% of quota 1989, 1990, 1991.
- Developed nomination and selection process for accounts in the portfolio, worldwide, national and local implementation.
- Created and instituted industry specific and general business plans for sales area portfolio accounts.
- Designed strategy to address and resolve account management conflicts for both direct and indirect sales channels.

NATIONAL ACCOUNTS DISTRICT SALES MANAGER   1987 - 1988
TERRITORY ACCOUNTS
Complete profit and loss responsibility for all national accounts in the territory.
- Achieved 121% of quota.
- Increased customer satisfaction rating in accounts portfolio 40% via customer involvement and followup.
- Generated area operating plan for key account strategy and revenue achievement.

AREA STRATEGIC SALES MANAGER   1986 - 1987
Responsible for development and execution of sales strategies representing the Area Sales Vice President.
* Developed and executed sales strategies resulting in $57M in new business.
* Designed and delivered training for identification and closure of strategic sales opportunities for all industries.

CHANNELS SALES MANAGER   1984 -1986
Created a business plan, developed sales strategies and managed resources to penetrate channels marketplace.
* Managed Florida/Georgia channels sales group achieving 171% of quota.
* Built and executed business plan to stabilize and revitalize channels accounts portfolio.
* Recruited and negotiated with a significant number of value added resellers to transfer their solution to Digital's platforms.

SALES MANAGER   1983 - 1984
Generated a business plan to implement sales strategies to enhance current customers and new accounts base.
* Transformed last place sales branch to top sales branch in 1984. Achieved 132% of quota.
* Improved entire sales branch to 100% plus of quota with four (4) sales representatives being in top 10% of U.S. sales force.
* Generated over twenty-five (25) new accounts, the majority being competitive replacements.

SALES EXECUTIVE   1981 - 1983
* Achieved 220% of quota.
* Developed and implemented large computer group business plan.
* Sold systems to a wide variety of industries and applications.

SENIOR SALES REPRESENTATIVE   1978 - 1981
Created and launched first government systems group sales plan for state of Florida.
* Opened largest number of new accounts in the territory.
* Supervised a combined end user/channels' territory with emphasis on building new accounts base.

SERVICETEK   1968 - 1978
Full service computer company

ACCOUNT MANAGER, COMPUTER SYSTEMS   1973 - 1978
* Major Accounts Manager.
* Developed and executed business plan to increase market share and revenue.

SYSTEMS MANAGER/SYSTEMS REPRESENTATIVE   1968 - 1973
* Extensive systems and applications knowledge in Medical, Government, Education, General Accounting and Manufacturing.
* In depth consulting and project management experience.

EDUCATION

B.S., Business - University of Tennessee
Extensive managerial and technical training courses and seminars

Name
Address
Phone Number

OBJECTIVE

A position in sales leading to a management opportunity.

SUMMARY

Experienced Sales Manager in the metals industry with achievements in increasing sales and market penetration, budget planning and control, sales training, and knowledge of end users and markets. Key strengths in problem solving, team building, leadership and motivation, computer literate in Lotus 1-2-3, DBase, and WordPerfect.

PROFESSIONAL EXPERIENCE

ALUMINUM INCORPORATED   1982 - 1993
A leading domestic producer of common alloy sheet and plate products.

Regional Sales Manager - Dallas	1990 - 1993
District Sales Manager - Dallas	1985 - 1990
Area Manager - St. Louis	1982 - 1985

INDUSTRIAL ALUMINUM CORP.   1974 - 1982
A leading producer of aluminum sheet and plate, extrusions, foil and containers, ingot and billet, forgings, and rod, bar and wire products.

Senior Sales Representative - St. Louis	1980 - 1982
Branch Sales Manager - Spokane	1978 - 1980
Extrusion Specialist - Chicago	1976 - 1978
Sales Associate - Cleveland	1975 - 1976
Customer Service Rep./Sales Trainee - Baltimore	1974 - 1975
Sales Trainee - Atlanta	1974

CAREER HIGHLIGHTS

- Rebuilt neglected sales territory from 350,000 pounds per year to over 15,000,000 pounds per year.

- Initiated and nurtured major truck trailer account becoming a major supplier one year after initial order.

- Increased sales and market penetration within region, bringing in 64 new accounts and increasing total sales by 111% within 6 years, through effective team building and territory restructuring.

- Reduced claim resolution time by 84% on 95% of claims by writing and introducing a new claims policy for six plants and field sales.

- Conducted sales training course for field sales, customer service, and technical personnel to promote selling and communication skills, providing a common language and skill improvement.

- Planned and managed annual regional sales budget in excess of $100,000. Region was never over budget.

- Managed sales team which exceeded sales goals 7 of last 8 years.

MILITARY

United States Navy, Submarine Service, E-4   1968 - 1971

EDUCATION

Georgia State University - 1974
BBA Marketing (minor statistics)
Learning International, Professional Selling Skills-Certified Instructor - 1992
Dale Carnegie, Effective Speaking - 1979
Karras, Effective Negotiating - 1976
Xerox, Professional Selling Skills - 1976

Name
Address
Phone Number

OBJECTIVE

To teach in an elementary school in a regular classroom environment or in the gifted area of special education.

SUMMARY

Ten years experience as a classroom teacher, ranging in grades 1-8, both gifted and regular students. Enjoy creating a learning environment and have been rewarded with excellent student relations.

PROFESSIONAL ACCOMPLISHMENTS

• Increased the enrollment of gifted students by 5% of school population through in-depth testing and evaluation, and teacher-parent surveys.

• Wrote proposal for school computer lab resulting in the implementation of a reading and math school-based computer lab.

• Developed a curriculum guide for the gifted and talented program which was used in the classroom.

• Created the first school newspaper as a means for student and faculty to publish different types of writings.

• Served as Teacher-Consultant for the National Writing Project, conducting writing in-service workshops to teachers in all grades, covering all academic areas.

• Served on Board of Directors for the Louisiana Chapter of the National Writing Project, arranging schedules for project meetings, activities and workshops.

• Designed a mid-term report card which was used in summer school sessions.

• Supervised fund-raising campaigns and academic activities as BETA Club sponsor, which raised over $500 dollars.

• Assisted in organization of elementary curriculum while serving as member of Blue Ribbon Committee for Excellence.

PROFESSIONAL EXPERIENCE

MIDDLE SCHOOL - Baton Rouge, Louisiana   **1987 - Present**

<u>Talented and Gifted Teacher, Grades 5-8</u>
Designed a curriculum to incorporate social studies, writing, English, and language arts skills into four main categories of study - Creativity, Research, Computer Study and Critical Thinking Skills. Students developed well rounded and practical application of skills.

CENTER PRIMARY SCHOOL - Baton Rouge, Louisiana   **1986 - 1987**

<u>Talented and Gifted Teacher, Grades 1-4</u>
Introduced an enrichment curriculum to enhance the students' courses of study. Resulted in students increased creativity and self-expression.

ST. PAUL ELEMENTARY - Baton Rouge, Louisiana   **1981 - 1986**

<u>Regular Classroom Teacher, Grade 1</u>
Taught all academic areas, including math, science, social studies, language arts, reading and physical education.

NORTH ELEMENTARY SCHOOL - Columbia, Missouri   **1980 - 1981**

<u>Regular Classroom Teacher, Grade 1</u>
Taught all academic areas, including math, science, social studies, language arts and reading.

SOUTHWEST ELEMENTARY SCHOOL - Columbia, Missouri   **Summer, 1980**

<u>Regular Classroom Teacher, Grades 3 and 4</u>
Taught math and English in nine-week summer session.

EDUCATION

Master in Education, 1988
Louisiana State University, Baton Rouge, Louisiana
Major: Elementary Education

Bachelor of Science Degree, 1980
Stark State College, Columbia, Missouri
Major: Elementary Education
Minor: Guidance and Counseling

Certification in Gifted, 1988
Louisiana State University, Baton Rouge, Louisiana

Name
Address
Phone Number

OBJECTIVE

Responsible education position in an independent school district.

SUMMARY

Twenty years in regular and special education instruction. Certification for Elementary and Language and/or Learning Disabilities.

Key strengths include:

- Use of computers to improve efficiency and effectiveness of student documentation and lesson plans.
- Exceptional understanding of parents' and students' needs.
- Consistently rated at or near the maximum score on the Texas Teacher Appraisal System.
- Workshop presentation and adult education.

Respected for professionalism as a leader by peers, administrators and school board members. Awarded Teacher of the Year for the school district.

PROFESSIONAL EXPERIENCE

HOMER SCHOOL DISTRICT - Homer, Texas   **1975 - 1990**

<u>Resource Teacher</u>, Special Education   1978 - 1990

<u>First Grade Teacher</u>   1975 - 1978

- Developed computerized program for writing Individualized Education Plans and daily lesson plans. Reduced preparation time by 50%.

- Demonstrated use and application of computerized IEP's to Houston's Regional Education Center. Alvin ISD purchased a computerized IEP program applicable to all grade levels and all subjects. The entire special education staff began using computerized IEP's.

- Developed a Scope and Sequence for an entire special education curriculum, grades 1-3 as well as a flow chart for each six weeks. This process was then introduced to the district special education instructors.

- Developed computerized grade book to document students' mastery of basic skills. Individual skills were scored and easily tracked on a one page document.

- Participated in a "train the trainer" seminar on delivery of Language Arts methods. Conducted a variety of workshops in local districts. Developed expertise in delivery of the following subjects: Classroom and Behavior Management, Temperament styles, Spelling methods and Whole language activities.

- Served on three district committees to develop a five year plan for TEA in problem solving, special education and district philosophy. Plan was completed on schedule and accepted by TEA.

- Proposed salary alternatives to the School Board as well as incentive pay plans to reward good attendance and suggestions from the employees. Suggestions were approved by the school board and are currently being investigated by the administration.

- Represented campus at monthly District Communications meetings with the Superintendent to help improve communication between administration and teachers.

BENTLEY SCHOOL DISTRICT - Hudson, New York   **1974 - 1975**
<u>Departmentalized Teacher</u>, Special Education

WAKE FOREST SCHOOL DISTRICT - Dallas, Texas   **1971 - 1974**
<u>Resource Teacher</u>, Special Education   1973 - 1974

<u>Fourth Grade Teacher</u>   1971 - 1974

CENTRAL SCHOOL DISTRICT - Dallas, Texas   **1970 - 1971**
<u>Remedial Reading Teacher</u>

EDUCATION/PROFESSIONAL TRAINING

Advanced Academic Training, 90 hours, TEA approved, 1986-1989

Thomas University, Houston, Texas, 1984-1986
Graduate courses on Learning Styles

Alvin Community College, Alvin, Texas, 1981
Computer Programming course

Sam Houston State University, Huntsville, Texas
Graduate Special Education Courses, 1976-1977
Special Education Certification, 1973

B.S., Elementary Education, North Texas State University, Denton, Texas, 1970

PROFESSIONAL ASSOCIATIONS

Association of Texas Professional Educators

Association for Children with Learning Disabilities, member
Association for Retarded Citizens, member
Bay Area Reading Council, member
Texas Reading Association, member

ACTIVITIES

- Directed one of the Adult Education programs in a local church for a three year period after assisting for three years and attending a series of nine courses to be certified as a Minister of Adult Education. Scheduled and taught weekly classes for 10-20 adults.

- Conducted a program on forgiveness to a group of 50 members of a support group for divorced and widowed men and women. Received positive feedback and was invited to return.

- Served on Board of Directors to form a "Third-Age Learning Center" with activities twice a week for Senior Citizens in a 30-mile radius. Contacted area merchants and businesses for potential classes then developed the curriculum and schedule for the first two semesters. Over 30 participants completed the first semester and it has grown to nearly 100 participants!

- Coordinated efforts of two organizations to write and distribute a monthly community newsletter. Newsletter was distributed to 3,000 boxholders monthly.

5
LETTERS FOR EVERY SITUATION

OVERVIEW

Letters are powerful, useful tools in your job search. To work well, however, they need to be well-written and look professional, matching your resumé. They must also have correct spelling, punctuation, and grammar, present your ideas well and clearly, be in the proper format, and accurately show names, addresses, and titles.

The effectiveness of marketing letters can also be greatly enhanced—doubling or trebling your response rate—by a telephone follow-up a day or two after the letter is received. In this way, you will register an impression and perhaps get an interview before the letter is lost in the pile and forgotten. You will need to take this into account when you plan the rate of issuing broadcast letters (identical letters sent to different companies/individuals). There is a limit to the number of letters you can follow up by phone (perhaps 20 or 30 a week).

The effectiveness of letter writing can be roughly evaluated by the number of interviews obtained per hundred letters sent out. As a rule of thumb, a yield of 1 to 2 percent is fair; a 10 percent yield is spectacular.

REASONS FOR WRITING

You use a *cover* letter whenever you send your resumé to someone. This includes answering an advertisement or posting, forwarding materials to a person who has asked for a resumé, or trying to encourage the opening of a new position for you at a company.

You also send a letter after you have had an interview, to *thank the interviewer*. This courtesy sets you apart from the average job seeker and keeps your name in the interviewer's mind. It also allows you to add or correct any information that might help you to be more favorably considered for the job.

You may wish to *send* your resumé to executive search agencies. This special submission requires you to present your skills persuasively enough to stand out among the flood of resumés they receive, and provide the special information which they require to meet their clients' needs.

When you receive a desirable offer, you need to *confirm your acceptance* in writing, assuring your new employer that you will report and documenting offer conditions to avoid possible confusion and later disappointment.

After you have found a job, you then need to call or write to your references, your network, and any companies or organizations who may be considering you for a job to thank them for their time, help, and/or consideration. This not only sustains your professional image, but helps *maintain your relationships* for future contacts.

The Structure of a Basic Cover Letter

Your own individually prepared letters will be most effective for displaying your capabilities. However, not everyone feels comfortable writing such potentially important letters. Also, you may need to get the letter out quickly and wish to minimize the time required to compose your own letters.

Accordingly, sample letters are included in this chapter which can greatly simplify the process, should you be able to use a standardized format. And it's always helpful to get someone to take a look at your letter(s) anyway. You know what you want to say, but someone else can tell you if you succeeded.

You should organize your letters, particularly cover letters, using the FOSH Formula, which contains three simple elements:

FO is to FOcus the reader's attention on why the letter is being sent. This gives perspective and allows the reader to evaluate information related to his or her needs. Don't apply for two unrelated jobs in the same letter—you will seem less interested and qualified for either. It is usually helpful to provide the source of your response, so the reviewer can put your application in context, and *vital* to do so when your source gives you any advantage, including an internal referral and its implied endorsement.

You might also use various techniques to "hook" the reader, grabbing his/her attention. Methods include: (1) Use "you" or "your" more often than "I", "me," or "my." (2) Use the name of a mutual acquaintance. (3) Ask a relevant question. (4) Compliment the reader or the reader's company or organization. (5) Make an interesting, but relevant, observation. (6) Refer to a recent news item concerning the reader or the company. (7) Request advice or assistance.

S is to Sell yourself by relating those characteristics which meet job requirements. Specific claims of capabilities are usually necessary, as screening normally compares applicants' skills and knowledge against job requirements. Just selling your overall capabilities is not usually helpful, because it does not allow the reader to determine whether your job experience qualifies you for the position.

If your letter is being sent in response to an advertisement, you will need to have analyzed the ad to see what skills and experience are required. Point out those skills or that experience which directly responds to the ad's requirements. Be specific and complete. Do not merely state "see resumé." If an employer is asking for some skill or experience that you have that is not mentioned in your resumé, you might mention that it is not in the resumé but that you have it and when and where you acquired it.

If an employer wants a skill or experience you do not have, then you have several choices: (1) show how you can quickly acquire it; (2) show how you can do the job without it (but do not suggest that it is an unimportant or irrelevant skill); or (3) ignore it. Where the first two choices are not relevant, you may ignore responding to the requirement, hoping few applicants have all the skills listed, the reviewer fails to notice the omission, or the need is not particularly important. Any of these could keep you under consideration.

H ends the letter with Housekeeping items: thanking the reviewer for consideration, suggesting an interview, noting inclusion of a resumé, and providing any contact information (where to telephone, for example). Some assertiveness is warranted, along with assumptions or suggestions for positive action to encourage arrangements for an interview or other next step.

It is generally better to maintain control ("I look forward to discussing my qualifications with you."), but stop short of annoying the reader ("I will call you next week to determine the best steps," not: "I will stop by Tuesday at 9:00 A.M."). Indicate your appreciation for being considered or for the time given for review, advice, or assistance ("Thank you for your consideration.").

THE FORMAT OF A BASIC BUSINESS LETTER

Business letters are typically written in fairly rigid formats which must be followed to avoid negative evaluation of your correspondence. Some flexibility exists in layout and style, but virtually all letters require:

1. Your name and address at the top. This is probably identical to your resumé, but if you need to add a message telephone number or fax, you may do so;
2. The date;
3. An address block, beginning with "Mr.," "Ms.", or if the addressee's sex is unknown, "M.," and the title, followed by the organization and then the full mailing address. Try to avoid writing just to a function (e.g., "Attention: Human Resources Manager") or similar approaches;
4. A greeting, beginning: "Dear Mr." or "Dear Ms." and the person's family name. If you do not know the person's sex—perhaps only initials are known or his or her first name does not identify the sex, such as Jean or Dana—address: "Dear M." and the last name. If you know the person you are writing is female and whether she is married, you can use "Miss" or "Mrs." instead of "Ms". If you cannot get a name, use: "Dear Sir or Madam," "Dear Human Resources Professional," "Dear Hiring Authority," or a similar title. Avoid "To whom it may concern"; and
5. Ample room between the closing "Sincerely," and your printed name, for your signature.

More important items include the following:

- You may list "Encl." to show you have included your resumé. You may also show initials and those of the typist ("XXXaa"), but this practice is no longer required, and is usually omitted.
- Your resumé should be neatly and clearly copied on bond paper (with watermark). The color may be white, cream, or beige, but avoid extreme colors or gray (copies from gray paper appear smudged).
- The letter should be printed on the same bond as the resumé.
- A business letter envelope of the same bond stock should be addressed with the same information as the letter's address block. The return address should be typed, but a simple stick-on label may be used. If matching bond envelopes are unavailable, a plain paper envelope of the same color may be used without reducing the impression, as envelopes are normally discarded.
- The letter should be stacked on top of the resumé, not stapled to it, folded a third up from the bottom, then the top third folded down, and inserted in the envelope.
- Use a "spellcheck" program and proofread. Any errors frequently disqualify candidacy immediately.
- Use the correct name, properly spelled, and the correct title and address of recipient.
- When responding to a blind box ad, send a similarly addressed letter ("Box

Number _____" and "Dear Sir or Madam") if necessary. If you can, research to obtain a clearer address, the Post Office must disclose box number holders.

- Do not use abbreviations, acronyms, or jargon. It's always safer to use language most people understand. Write your letter as if your reader knows very little about the work you do.
- Don't identify or refer to your own personal characteristics, such as age or sex. Don't refer to age or sex-based conditions, such as "slowing down."
- Avoid outdated phrases, such as "Yours truly," "pursuant to," "in regards to," "the undersigned," etc.
- Center your text on the page—don't jam a letter into the top portion.
- You can select virtually any "style"—block, indented, date and signature on left or right. Block is the simplest.

You need to be both complete and brief in responding. In all but extreme cases, your letter should not exceed one page.

PREPARING A THANK-YOU LETTER

Thank you letters are always sent to interviewers on the day following the interview. They are also usually sent to those who provided networking information, advice, or other assistance. The same "FOSH" approach is effective for these letters as in writing cover letters, allowing you to enhance your position.

Many candidates will fail to send letters, allowing your correspondence to make you appear better qualified. Yours should show your business acumen, demonstrate your writing skill, clarify any outstanding issues, add important qualifications, express your appreciation for the interview, and reiterate or suggest next action steps.

A standard business letter format is usual for acknowledging most interviews. In rare circumstances (e.g., if interviewing away from home and typing is unavailable), a hand-written note is acceptable.

Send an original letter to each interviewer. The contents may be similar, but personalized. Do not send one letter with copies to others. Assume that they will be exchanged and read by each other, but may contain similar statements which apply to each person.

Thank-you letters begin by conveying your thanks, normally adding, "for your time and interest in discussing the position of _____." You may then add clarifying comments which enhance your capability or show how you "fit" into the organization. You should end by reiterating your understanding of the next steps or indicating what you will do next. You might close by restating your appreciation.

PREPARING AN EXECUTIVE SEARCH FIRM APPLICATION LETTER

Forwarding your resumé to an Executive Search Firm requires a cover letter that makes you a candidate for potential future searches, provides salary and preferred location conditions, and recognizes the processes of such firms so they can effectively consider you. These firms recognize that the hiring organization is the client and you are the subject. Most will not find jobs for you, even though they may treat you professionally and pleasantly, but will try to find candidates for their clients' jobs. You also need to present yourself positively so that you will remain in contention to compete successfully with the literally hundreds of others who apply. If you are responding to a particular opening which is being recruited by an Executive Search Firm, you should follow the guidelines of a usual cover letter noted in the previous section. The standard business letter format is required.

You need to FOcus your letter, beginning by expressing that you wish to be considered for upcoming openings, and the field and level you are qualified to fill. You may wish to use similar "hooks" in writing to search firms as noted in Section I, under FOcus, including: (1) Compliment the firm's reputation; (2) Use the name of any referral; (3) Refer to news items; and (4) Make interesting observations. You may then wish to Sell yourself by listing some accomplishments or traits.

For Search Firm transmittals only, in the Housekeeping section you will need to provide pay information and relocation restrictions. Search firms must know your pay level and/or requirements to respond to their hiring organization clients and will not consider you unless they know. You are relatively protected for later bargaining even though you disclose this information to the Search Firm, as the hiring firm's compensation is normally a percent of new salary. The Search Firm normally recommends an offer level which is commensurate with your skills.

Virtually all search firms require personal observation of candidates before referring them to clients. They state that they interview all applicants so they know who to refer and will need to meet you to insure you qualify. However, in practice they cannot see even a fraction of those who apply.

To satisfy their ambiguous requirements you should state that you recognize that the recruiter will want to meet you, and you will call to arrange a suitable time. You should then expect that when you phone you will be denied a meeting, but should use the contact to attempt to favorably impress the firm, trying to have your resumé retained for future retrieval and referral.

PREPARING AN OFFER CONFIRMATION LETTER

You should commit your acceptance of an offer to writing, confirming when you are expected to start and obligating your new organization to you. You may further wish to clarify or confirm the particular offer conditions.

When an offer has been made in writing and the conditions have been clearly indicated, you may respond with a brief letter merely referring to the offer. However, when an offer is only oral, or where the offer letter failed to provide important conditions, you need to confirm your understanding to avoid confusion and problems. This letter should detail all important conditions, including salary, the time period for which the salary is calculated (monthly, weekly, etc.), hours of work, benefits, review or promotion promises and amounts, any special conditions, and perhaps job assignments, duties, or responsibilities.

You also need to write a letter either rejecting any offer you decline or confirming your rejection. You should be careful to retain as positive a relationship as possible— you may again be a candidate.

The standard business letter format is required. You should take special care to leave a positive impression, including expressing your satisfaction with the circumstances and your eagerness to join such a fine organization.

Once you've accepted an offer, you need to call or write all of your supporters, references, network contacts, organizations considering you, and agencies which have your resumé.

You have an option of using your own stationery, or, with your new firm's approval to use the new company stationery, to notify supporters. The standard business letter format is still required, although you should be informal with those you know well. Your supporters should be thanked, and you should indicate your reaction to the new job. Be sure you provide your new business location, telephone, and fax.

NORMAN MAINE
31444 Business Street
Winamucka , WA 12345
Home: (818) 123-4567
Message: (818) 972-2695

September 29, 1995
Mr. Mark Smith
Vice President
ABC Bank
123 Main Street
Anytown, NY 11111

Dear Mr. Smith *(or First Name, if appropriate)*:

During a recent conversation I had with Skip Browning, he suggested you as a person who could provide me with some valuable information and advice.

I recently became a casualty of the Peninsula National/Equitable merger in Baltimore. With my strong record, I would like to stay in banking, preferably in the Baltimore-Washington area. It would be most helpful to review this objective with you.

I do not expect you to have a position for me or to know where one might be available.   However, enclosed is a copy of my credentials, which outlines my qualifications and a partial list of what I believe I could contribute to a financial institution.

Realizing the demands on your time, I will give you a call the week of February 5th to see if a brief meeting would be possible.

Thank you, in advance, for your interest and thoughts.

Sincerely,

Norman Maine

Encl.

NORMAN MAINE
31444 Business Street
Winamucka , WA 12345
Home: (818) 123-4567
Message: (818) 972-2695

October 13, 1995
Mr. John Smith
President
XYZ Corporation
123 Broadway
Richmond, CT 06000

Dear John *(First Name would be appropriate at this point):*

Thank you for taking the time on Tuesday to discuss the Manufacturer's Representative business with me. Your knowledge of the industry and your suggestions have provided me with a new and interesting career possibility to consider.

The hands-on operation of the business and the opportunity to maintain my contacts and relationships make it a very exciting possibility.

I will continue to conduct my research on various industries and will begin to narrow my focus in the coming months. My interest in your new Tool and Equipment Division is a subject I would like to explore further with you.

Once again, thank you for your interest and your willingness to assist me. I will call you after my meeting with Mr. Lewis.

Sincerely,

Norman Maine

NORMAN MAINE
31444 Business Street
Winamucka, WA 12345
Home: (818) 123-4567
Message: (818) 972-2695

September 29, 1995

Mr. Waldo Lydecker
Human Resources Recruiter
Management Technology, Inc.
1234 W. Adams Blvd.
Pico Rivera, CA 91499

Dear Mr. Lydecker:

My interest is for the position of _____ at your organization. I
have strong experience which I believe qualifies me to perform that job. My background is
provided in the attached resumé.

I look forward to discussing my qualifications with you. Please call me at the number noted
above and I will arrange to see you at your convenience.

Sincerely,

Norman Maine

Encl.

NOTE: If you have problems with writing, but need something to transmit a resumé, you can use
this, substituting only the name and address, and inserting the job advertised or listed.

NORMAN MAINE
31444 Business Street
Winamucka, WA 12345
Home: (818) 123-4567
Message: (818) 972-2695

September 29, 1995

M. Im Jung Kwuon
Human Resources
The Megaprofit Corp.
1234 W. Adams Blvd.
Pico Rivera, CA 91499

Dear M. Kwuon:

I am interested in the **(describe job sought)** job which **(note how you heard of it - advertisement, employee referral, listing)**.

My strong experience in **(describe your experience in those areas which the job opening announcement requires)** is an excellent match for your needs. Additionally, I have **(note two accomplishments doing the work sought which are <u>not</u> on resumé)**.

Enclosed is my resumé for your further consideration. I look forward to discussing my skills and experience with you, and will call you in a few days to arrange a satisfactory time.

Sincerely,

Norman Maine

Encl.

> **NOTE:** If you are somewhat uncomfortable writing, but wish to sell yourself a bit, and can present some of your background, insert pertinent information in this format.

NORMAN MAINE
31444 Business Street
Winamucka, WA 12345
Home: (818) 123-4567
Message: (818) 972-2695

September 16, 1992

Mr. Waldo Lydecker
Human Resources Recruiter
Management Technology, Inc.
1234 W. Adams Blvd.
Pico, WA 91499

Dear Mr. Lydecker:

Thank you for your consideration during my interview. The information you provided was most helpful.

I am very interested in employment with your organization, and I hope I provided you sufficient background to allow you to consider my skills.

You may reach me at the telephone noted above. Thank you again for your time.

Sincerely,

Norman Maine

NOTE: This letter is minimally acceptable to express your appreciation for the interview.

NORMAN MAINE
31444 Business Street
Winamucka, WA 12345
(818) 123-4567

December 29, 1995

Mr. Arlington Spangler Brugh
Vice President
Management Search, Inc.
12344 West Marine Blvd.
Searchlight, CA 91233

Dear Mr. Brugh:

My career at **ABC Company** is ending as the general decline in aerospace has reached my group.

I am now ready for a senior level engineering or project management position with a future opportunity to move into general management in a substantial firm.

My current salary is in the $70,000 range, but I recognize the current economic conditions, and, because I am primarily interested in a challenging position, would consider the mid-$60,000 level. Even a bit of risk—such as a turnaround situation—would be acceptable if an equity arrangement were offered. I am willing to relocate for the right assignment.

As you will notice from the enclosed resumé, my commercial and governmental experience has given me a strong and varied background.

I recognize that you may not have a current search assignment that fits my objectives, and many other potential candidates are also contacting you. However, I believe I have some very marketable skills, and would still appreciate the chance to chat with you. Accordingly, I will call you in a few days to arrange a mutually satisfactory time. Management Search has always had my highest respect.

Sincerely,

Norman Maine

Enclosure

NOTE: It is necessary to break the rules by mentioning location limitations and salary or salary expectations to address a search consultant's needs. Additionally, most executive search consultants wish to know candidates personally before referring them, so suggest an interview and note you will request one. However, expect that few will actually consent to interview. Recognition of the search process aids candidacy. Some assertiveness may increase both present interest and retention for future searches. Complimenting the Search Firm can't hurt.

NORMAN MAINE
31444 Business Street
Winamucka, WA 12345
(818) 123-4567

September 29, 1995

Mr. Waldo Lydecker
Human Resources Recruiter
Management Technology, Inc.
1234 W. Adams Blvd.
Chicago, IL 54321

Dear Mr. Lydecker:

Thank you for your consideration during our discussion regarding the _____ job. I also appreciated your descriptions (**of** _____), and found the information most helpful.

As we discussed the (**describe the topic you wish to clarify or expand on**), I thought I should have provided clarification, but the conversation moved on. However, (**insert what you want to add - some work you've done well; an accomplishment; the clarification**).

I am very interested in employment with (**Name of Company**), and I hope I provided you with sufficient background to evaluate my skills.

You may reach me at the telephone number noted above. Thank you again for your time (**if you wish to be more assertive, add: I look forward to working for you**).

Sincerely,

Norman Maine

NOTE: This letter must be completed to provide additional information, and may allow you to correct interview misstatements or improve your candidacy by describing additional capabilities.

NORMAN MAINE
31444 Business Street
Winamucka, WA 12345
Home: (818) 123-4567

July 4, 1995

Ms. Laura Michaelson
Director, Customer Relations
The XYZ Corporation
9145 South "F" Street
St. Regis, FL 16257

Dear Ms. Michaelson:

You were very informative during my interview on June 19th. The job is appealing, and XYZ Corporation is clearly a good place to work.

In the interim since the interview, I have reviewed my capabilities and the job requirements, and am convinced that I can do an excellent job for you. Particularly, **(insert one of your skills, knowledge, or traits, and relate it to a job requirement).**

I presume you are still considering me, and I am very interested in joining you. I hope you can contact me soon to proceed **(if you wish to be more assertive, add: or I will contact you at the end of the week).**

Thank you for your consideration, and I look forward to a productive association.

Sincerely,

Norman Maine

NOTE: This letter allows you to add additional information which may improve your candidacy by showing how your capabilities can contribute to the job. It also may resurrect your application, and gives you the opportunity to reassume control by calling for information if you are not contacted.

NORMAN MAINE
31444 Business Street
Winamucka, CA 12345
Home: (818) 123-4567
Message: (818) 972-2695

December 11, 1995

Mr. Archibald Leech
Manager, Product Development Department
Huey Dewey Company
123 Industrial Way
Commerce, CA 12345

Dear Mr. Leech:

I am pleased to accept your offer of employment to work for Huey Dewey Company. The arrangements you outlined in your letter of December 9, 1995 are quite satisfactory.

I am excited about the opportunities and working with you and your staff, and I look forward to joining you on December 19.

Sincerely,

Norman Maine

NOTE: This letter is applicable when offer conditions have been carefully and completely delineated in a written offer.

Ms. Tula Finklea
2323 Lavender Lane
Carnation, NJ 91344
Home: (818) 123-4567
Message: (818) 972-2695

December 10,1995

Ms. Edith Marriner
Manager, Office Services
ABC Corporation
123 E. Anywhere Street
Big City, MD 11111

Dear Ms. Marriner:

I am pleased to accept the position of Word Processing Operator which we discussed last week. The following is my understanding of our mutual agreement:

- Start date will be Monday, December 15, 1995

- Salary will be $15.00 per hour for a 40-hour work week.

- The work shift will be from 8:00 a.m. to 5:00 p.m., with one hour for lunch. Any overtime will be compensated at 1-1/2 times the hourly rate, or $22.50 per hour.

- I am entitled to two weeks vacation per year, which will be increased to three weeks if I am promoted to supervisor. Unused vacation will carry over.

I look forward to starting work on December 15, and joining ABC.

Sincerely,

Tula Finklea

NOTE: This letter may show the form of address to clarify gender when names or initials may not so identify.

Ms. Tula Finklea
2323 Lavender Lane
Carnation, NJ 91344
Home: (818) 123-4567
Message: (818) 972-2695

December 15, 1995

Ms. Norma J. Baker
Manager, Office Services
DEF Corporation
456 Somewhere Court
Big City, MD 11111

Dear Ms. Baker:

I appreciate the time you took to interview me for the position in your word processing department. I was impressed with the efficiency of your operation and the friendliness of the staff.

As I mentioned on the phone the other day, the position you offered does not match my skills or salary requirement, so I reluctantly must turn it down. I hope that you will keep me in mind if other positions open, particularly ones involving greater responsibility and supervisory duties.

Sincerely,

Tula Finklea

HUEY DEWEY COMPANY
123 Industrial Way
Commerce, NM 12345
(818) 567-9089
FAX: (818) 567-9099

September 16, 1995

Mr. Samuel Sneed
1234 W. Golf Blvd.
Rancho Mirage, CA 91499

Dear Sammy:

Thank you for all your support during my job search. I have decided to join The Huey Dewey Company, and will start next (started last) week as _____. I'm excited about the opportunity, and will let you know how things are going. I am enclosing my new business card.

Thanks again for your help. I couldn't have done it without you. I'll call you in a couple of weeks when I'm settled.

Sincerely,

Norman Maine

NM:ld

NOTE: You may, with permission, use new Company stationery. If you do not, and do not yet have a business card to forward, you should include your new address and telephone number. The addressee's title and company may be added where appropriate.

NORMAN MAINE
31444 Business Street
Winamucka, WA 12345
Home: (818) 123-4567
Message: (818) 972-2695

September 16, 1995

Mr. Waldo Lydecker
Human Resources Recruiter
Management Technology, Inc.
1234 W. Adams Blvd.
Cleveland, OH 12345

Dear Mr. Lydecker:

Thank you for considering me for employment. I have decided to accept another offer, so must withdraw my application with you at this time.

I do appreciate your time, and hope I may contact you in the future should I again be looking for a new opportunity.

Sincerely,

Norman Maine

NOTE: This letter should be sent to companies who are *actively* considering you, including those where interviews or offers are pending, and perhaps to Search Firms.

WHERE TO GO FROM HERE

Target your search and track your efforts. Be sure your resumé and letters are suited to your target market. Selectively distribute your marketing materials to the people who can help you the most in your job search. Start by networking with people you know who work in your desired field. Make follow-up calls on a regular basis, and try to talk to as many people as possible.

Identify the companies that you'd like to work for and the organizations that have a need for your skills. Most public libraries have compendiums of corporations. Some, like the Dun & Bradstreet Directory, provide vital information that you'll need: addresses, phone numbers, names and titles of executives, and summaries of key products and markets. If you suspect that this information is not current or specific enough, call the company to make sure you're sending your resumé to the proper person. Get the correct spelling of the person's name, and doublecheck the address.

Many professional organizations have job banks. Use them. And don't overlook the organization's officers. Very often they know people throughout your field, and they know where the openings are. Use the increasing number of on-line resources described in chapter 2 to gather information on targeted organizations, and to broaden your access to desirable markets through resumé databases. These research and planning efforts up front will be reflected in your presentation materials, and will pay off as you begin to implement your job search.

Looking for a job is a continuous process that should never end—even after your search is over. Once you've landed a position, keep your network alive. Tell people where you are. Most of your network contacts will be interested in learning how your campaign turned out. Some of them were probably very involved in it and would appreciate your thanks. Make the effort to maintain this valuable network.

ABOUT THE EDITORS

BOB STIRLING is Group Vice President of the Career Transition Practice Area at Drake Beam Morin, Inc. Prior to joining DBM, Bob held a number of general management positions with IBM and was a pioneer in developing IBM's personal computer applications. With DBM, Bob has counseled a wide range of senior executives from insurance, banking, manufacturing, chemical, communication, retail, and government organizations.

PAT MORTON is Senior Vice President at Drake Beam Morin, Inc. She has served in senior management positions in human resources for more than 15 years with HBO (health care information systems) in Atlanta and Motorola in Dallas, Connecticut, and California. Pat currently serves on the faculty of New York University, teaching courses in Human Resources and Training Measurement and Starting a Career in Human Resources.

ABOUT DRAKE BEAM MORIN, INC.

Drake Beam Morin, Inc. is the world's leading career consulting firm. As experts in outplacement and internal career management, DBM consults daily with major corporations, private enterprises, not-for-profit organizations and governments around the world. With a network of nearly two hundred offices and thousands of consulting experts worldwide, DBM presents an almost limitless resource of up-to-the-minute information in the critical management science areas of careers and change.

From this uniquely rich resource base, DBM Publishing brings to the public material that incorporates this experience, lending it a creditability that no other publisher can match. We are, in essence, what we do and we are committed to providing the best in quality books and materials to meet and exceed the needs of our readers.

LOOK FOR THESE OTHER FINE
DBM PUBLISHING TITLES

50 Winning Answers to Interview Questions
Everything You Need to Know to Prepare Yourself For the Job Interview ($10.95)
This indispensable guide gives you the knowledge essential to achieving success in any interview. It's the one book that takes you to both sides of the desk to find out exactly what the toughest interviewers in America's top companies want to know, what they will ask, and what they want to hear. *50 Winning Answers to Interview Questions* will help you to speak for yourself and secure the job you want.

The First Job Hunt Survival Guide ($11.95)
"An excellent guide for any college student or graduate who is entering the job market. Clearly written, well-organized and packed with the type of information every job-seeker needs."
—Kevin Harrington
    Director, Career Services
    Harvard University
    Graduate School of Education

From Stress to Strength
Achieving Wellness at Work and in Life ($11.95)
Here are proven strategies to identify the sources of stress and move beyond them, and to manage time and energy effectively for a more fulfilling, productive, and balanced life. Includes a personal stress assessment system.

Make Your Own Breaks
Become an Entrepreneur & Create Your Own Future ($15.95)
This savvy, step-by-step guide can help turn your entrepreneurial dreams into a profitable reality. With profiles of 40 top entrepreneurs, this book puts a world of money-making ideas and insights at your fingertips.

Stay in Control
How to Cope and Still Get the Job You Really Want ($14.95)
Hunting for a job requires complete focus, organization, and determination—which is precisely what you'll get from the numerous goal-oriented charts, exercises, and worksheets in *Stay in Control*. So, if you want to take charge and take control of your job search, this is one book you can't afford to ignore.

AVAILABLE AT ALL BOOKSTORES!